T0363816

ALMOST
INVINCIBLE

ALMOST INVINCIBLE

West Indies in England: 1984

RICHARD SYDENHAM

First published by Pitch Publishing, 2024

Pitch Publishing
9 Donnington Park,
85 Birdham Road,
Chichester,
West Sussex,
PO20 7AJ
www.pitchpublishing.co.uk
info@pitchpublishing.co.uk

A CIP catalogue record is available for this book
from the British Library.

ISBN 978 1 80150 687 8

Typesetting and origination by Pitch Publishing
Printed and bound in Great Britain by TJ Books, Padstow

Contents

Dedication

To the West Indies players of 1984 who inspired
me to watch and subsequently play cricket. Thanks
for the entertainment. I always wanted to write
this book as a tribute to the greatness that you
guys achieved that year, and in that era generally.

David Gower, thanks for your generosity and
honesty in reliving in detail this difficult summer
for you and England. Without your contribution,
this book would not have been anywhere near as
authentic.

My son Isaac, keep playing cricket and enjoying
it as much as I did when these great players from
1984 did their thing.

About the author

Richard Sydenham began his sports journalism career in 1994, writing predominantly on his beloved Aston Villa and Warwickshire CCC. He later freelanced for the *Sunday Telegraph* and news agencies such as Reuters and the Associated Press (AP), among many other outlets. In recent years he founded a sports management company, Big Star Creations, which looks after some of the world's leading cricketers as well as sourcing sporting speakers. Richard, who lives in Worcestershire – where he plays cricket on weekends – attributes his love of the sport to the West Indies team of 1984. This is his tenth book.

Author's Note

'Australia has "Bradman's Invincibles" and Steve Waugh's team of 2001/02 ... The West Indies deserve a legacy team or label that bossed all-comers ... don't they? My belief is the 1984 side, "Lloyd's Legends", is it. The best ever.'

It may seem peculiar for an Englishman to want to write this book, with passion and a thirst to learn more about what happened when the West Indies toured the British Isles in 1984, for it was an especially painful summer for the England cricket team.

I was only ten years old then but was still well aware that they – we – took one hell of a beating; 5-0 of course.

The thing is, that West Indies team was primarily responsible for my early fascination with this game. It wasn't unusual for the cricket to be on the tele at home during school holidays. Radio commentary sometimes provided background noise in the kitchen. Yes, Ian Botham and David Gower were national heroes by then and I wasn't averse to portraying them in backyard cricket with my brother, Jeff.

However, I was raised in a predominantly football-loving family and sporting passions in our household pretty much started and ended with the progress of Aston Villa. Even the exploits of our local county side,

Warwickshire, didn't register too much. It was all about Gary Shaw, Gordon Cowans, Tony Morley and Villa! We were champions of Europe in 1982, after all.

My casual enthusiasm for cricket changed in 1984. When Tony Barton made way for Graham Turner as manager of a Villa team that was descending into rapid decline, I found myself hypnotised by the West Indies.

These fellows ran in and terrorised our batsmen with pace and bounce like I'd never seen before. Their batsmen smashed England's bowlers with an abandon that was unlike the conservative brand of Test cricket I had known till then. And their fielders possessed an athleticism and ability to catch and throw that seemed unparalleled. I was hooked.

Maybe I should have been crying into my Sugar Puffs when we kept losing, match after match, but instead I felt an admiration and excitement for how the West Indies played.

I wasn't jumping ship – I still wanted England to win. I just wasn't as jingoistic in cricket as with football and Villa. It's still the case now. I rejoiced in early 1986 when listening to the *Test Match Special* radio commentary, every time we took a West Indies wicket or one of our batsmen managed a rare milestone. But I was able to appreciate the bigger picture.

Not like with football. When Arsenal beat Villa 6-2 at Villa Park and Tony Woodcock scored five there was no appreciation then, just scorn for our underperforming players and hatred for the Gunners. That wasn't the case with my growing love for the West Indies.

Gordon Greenidge and Desmond Haynes became my childhood heroes for many years. Malcolm Marshall and Joel Garner were my favourite fast bowlers. Was it coincidence that shortly after this period, my 'second' and 'third' county teams were Hampshire (Greenidge and Marshall) and Somerset (Garner, Viv Richards and Botham)? Certainly not.

Even the little things from that time bring me fond memories, such as collecting the Texaco-sponsored caricature (cigarette-packet style) cards from 1984. There were a dozen, six from each side: Greenidge, Marshall, Richards, Garner, Michael Holding and Clive Lloyd from the West Indies; Botham, Gower, Allan Lamb, Bob Willis, Derek Randall and Chris Tavare from England.

I was too old to collect Smurf figurines by then and was growing out of *Star Wars* too. This was something new and exciting. Even with the rare *Panini Cricket '83* sticker album, the West Indies player stickers seemed unique and special, as were England players like Botham, Gower, Graham Dilley and Mike Gatting.

In league cricket, I have mostly been an opening batsman from teenage years, and that was a result of the exhibitions of the Bajan pair Greenidge and Haynes. How ironic, then, that I became more of a Mike Atherton or Alastair Cook-type obdurate/dependable player than emulating the flamboyant stroke play of my heroes. But I won't bore you with the reasons!

Over time, I heard or read some observers insist how the West Indies were bad for the game – even boring – because their fast bowlers contravened the spirit of cricket by intimidating batsmen, they caused slow over rates, they were one-dimensional, they bypassed a specialist spin bowler (though not in 1984). Everyone is entitled to their view, but I thought such opinions were wide of the mark.

To me, those three or four West Indies express fast bowlers that came bounding in at batsmen created a fresh, exhilarating element to cricket. I always thought the challenge was on the batsman to find a way to succeed, rather than the challenge being on the West Indies to find a different way to win.

I always admired the ugly, gutsy, mongrel-type batsmen who played the quick bowlers well through sheer courage and determination. Allan Border, Steve Waugh, Robin Smith, Graeme Smith, Kepler Wessels. These guys found a way – they were my type of player. It might not have been pretty, but they found a method to survive and prosper.

It was one of England's failures in 1984 that not enough of their batsmen 'found a way', like Allan Lamb did. His way was to counter and throw punches. Chris Broad did reasonably well as a Test rookie, batting time and occupying the crease. The only problem with that tactic against this West Indies team was their hostility and excellence were relentless. One could hang around, though the scoreboard moved slowly, and the pressure only built rather than eroded.

My chief motivation for writing this book is to give kudos to one of the best cricket teams ever, if not *the* best there ever was. To learn more about them and their methods.

Australia has 'Bradman's Invincibles' of 1948 and Steve Waugh's team of 2001/02 time – the 'Mental Disintegrators' if you like – while England and India led the world briefly. But the West Indies had a whole generation of players that went undefeated in Test series from 1980 to 1995. Wicketkeeper Jeffrey Dujon played 81 Tests and never lost a single series. They deserve a legacy team or label that bossed all-comers … don't they?

My belief is the 1984 side is it. The best ever. Nitpickers might suggest West Indies had stronger teams, maybe with Andy Roberts and Colin Croft or Curtly Ambrose, Courtney Walsh and Patrick Patterson. It's subjective.

Yes, Larry Gomes, Roger Harper and Eldine Baptiste won't go down in history as *great* West Indies players, individually. But in this series, in 1984, they made vital contributions to possibly the most dominant Test series achievement we have ever seen. It's all about 'team' after all. The whole is greater than the sum of its parts.

Most players from both the West Indies and England sides of that summer seem to agree with me that these guys of 1984 were tops. Have a read and make up your own mind.

Foreword

by Ian Botham

When we talk about the story of the West Indies in 1984, we must remember this was one series within a 20-year period when they were comfortably the best side in the world. More importantly, this side in '84 was certainly the best side I ever played against and, I would argue, the best team there ever was. You don't get higher praise than that. They had all bases covered. Some have mentioned they never had a world-class spinner. But they didn't need one with the pace attack they had. They were amazing. If you managed a draw against them, you'd done exceptionally well, never mind a win, which were few and far between.

I see there is a chapter in here about our missing rebels in 1984. They would have made a difference but not very much. One or two would have had an impact but, in all honesty, it probably wouldn't have been enough of a difference to affect the series. This West Indies team was so professional, so methodical, and so well-drilled in every department. They had everything: strength in batting, they had great fast bowlers – and they really were fast – but with that you need great slip catchers and they had those, they took magnificent catches and didn't drop too many either. Their fielding generally was exceptional. There were no weaknesses.

It was David Gower's first series as the official England captain, and I knew all too well what kind of task he was facing because I had been there myself. Nine of my 12 matches as England Test captain, remember, were against this great team. Back then, the first thing I did at the end of a day's play was walk round the dressing room and see who was fit for tomorrow. Because they were formidable. Those series were tough enough and I thought we did well to only lose 1-0 at home (with four draws) and then 2-0 in the Caribbean (with two draws). Those scorelines certainly look a lot better than 5-0 and 5-0 (the 1984 and 1986 series results).

In 1984 with the advent of a new series against the West Indies, we all knew what was coming. I don't mean the scoreline, I'm referring to the challenge that lay ahead of us because when they came over, they brought an intent, a professionalism and, apart from anything else, just very good and talented athletes. Nothing that that side achieved surprised me because they were brilliant. Despite the obvious challenge facing us, I don't honestly believe that any England player went out there other than trying their absolute best and giving everything they had to the cause. I understand one or two have said in this book there was a lack of belief that we could beat the West Indies but, from my own point of view, I never felt like that in all my life.

Allan Lamb's record against them was as good as anyone's who played against the West Indies in that period. He must have had a fair bit of confidence and faith in himself. Negativity was never a part of my thinking. We dropped a few catches and didn't always do ourselves any favours in that regard, but I don't believe our lack of success was anything to do with self-belief.

This book will no doubt recall the moments when we had the West Indies on the ropes a few times that summer and although we couldn't finish them off, the fact we were in that position at all on several occasions, tells me we did pretty well. They always found a way to get out of trouble because that's how good and how professional they were. Ultimately, you can only go out there and compete and if you compete you never know what's going to happen. Anything is possible.

In terms of my own game, I had my moments (8-103 and 81 at Lord's in the second Test). I was given out lbw (on 81) and let's put it this way, if DRS was around then they wouldn't have looked at it very long. That was disappointing because I was batting well, and it just wasn't out. It was one of those things that happened and I had to move on, but not scoring a Test hundred against them was one of the few regrets of my career, though I did get a big hundred against them for Worcestershire. Quite simply though it was a tough, tough challenge. It was like facing a battering ram where the slowest of their fast bowlers was not much less than 90 miles per hour. Mikey, Maco, Joel, Patrick Patterson when he came on to the scene, they were just formidable and sometimes as a professional you had to accept the way things are at the times you play. It's professional sport, we tried very hard against them, we tried all kinds of tactics, and they were too good for us, though we did have our chances. I think back to my first Test as captain at Trent Bridge (in 1980), we should have beaten them then, but we dropped a couple of catches – David dropped a dolly that he would have taken 999 times out of a thousand – and lost by two wickets. These are the narrow margins of professional sport. It's ifs and buts. The fact of the matter is they were just a fantastic team.

There were some magnificent individual performances that summer. Viv's 189 not out at Old Trafford, for instance. One-dayers are different as you've only got so many overs you can bowl, there are field placing limitations, so it's slightly different but that innings was amazing. That was what Viv was capable of. In 1976, of course, he scored 829 runs in the series even though he missed the second Test! He was a genius, but obviously in a one-day international he had a bit more licence. Nine times out of ten we would have probably won that game, but it wasn't to be. Michael Holding hung around while Viv blitzed it. We all had our moments and that was certainly one of Viv's many moments in his career.

Gordon Greenidge's double century at Lord's was another incredible innings, after a declaration that David didn't have a lot of choice with. The chairman of selectors (Peter May) told him quite strongly that we had to go for it. We looked at each other in amazement because we had dug ourselves out of a hole and then the next minute we declared. We thought 'what's that all about?' It wouldn't happen nowadays. We all told David the pitch was flat, but Peter May put a lot of pressure on him. Once the West Indies cruised to victory, Peter wasn't to be seen at the end of the game.

That was as close as we came in 1984. But I reiterate, this was not any old team we were up against. They were incredible. Once they lost in Australia in 1975/76 and Clive Lloyd said 'we're not coming back here unless we have four or five fast bowlers' – from that point on, they were simply awesome. We know they went unbeaten in Test series for 15 years, but they hardly lost a match either. In the time (38 matches) between my first Test as captain (in 1980) and the end of this '84 series, they lost just once (to Australia in Melbourne in 1981).

We all know about the great names in that West Indies side – I've mentioned a few of them already – well, some of their best players in '84 were actually the unsung heroes like Eldine Baptiste, Roger Harper and Larry Gomes, who was one of the biggest thorns in our side. We would have them a few wickets down and yet Larry would be there, dogged, and score anything from 50 to over 100. He ground it out. So, they didn't all walk in and try to smack it. He was the steady general in the middle order. They even had players on the sidelines who weren't getting a game who would have got into any other Test side.

They were great, unbelievably good. Like I said, in my opinion they were the greatest ever. I'm not sure what Sir Donald Bradman would say about that as captain of the 'Invincibles' in 1948, but I know Australia didn't like Bodyline too much when England won (4-1). We had Bodyline for 20 years against this West Indies side! They were phenomenal and in many ways I consider myself lucky to have competed against possibly the best side that ever played the game.

Lord Ian Botham, March 2024.

'The team in 1984 is the best all-round side we ever had. We had everything. We had spin, we had pace, it was the best fielding team we ever had, our batting was strong. All bases were covered.' – Sir Clive Lloyd

'By the time the West Indian squad set off for Australia and five more Test matches from November (after the 1984 England series), there was a strong feeling of near invincibility.

'We had won our last eight Tests but, unlike the period when we lost to India in the 1983 World Cup Final, we were by no means complacent. We knew we were going to have to work hard to maintain our position as the best team in the world. Gone was the era of the calypso cricketer; we were now a tough, uncompromising group of players, hardened by battle and galvanised by the occasional failure.' – Malcolm Marshall

Background, West Indies: The Unstoppable Juggernaut

'There were so many great things about the side but perhaps the key was having a captain who didn't inhibit his players' natural talent and he encouraged us to express ourselves.' – Gordon Greenidge

The West Indies cricket team's global domination should be attributed to a clutch of world-class players who made them the champions they were in one-day and Test cricket. Great individuals came together and formed a great unit. But it was due in no small part to one man, Clive Lloyd.

Lloyd was a world-class batsman in his own right, but as captain he did so much for West Indies cricket that most leaders of other national teams did not have to concern themselves with. He was a diplomat first, for he fostered a strong unity among the various populations of Jamaica, Barbados, Antigua, Trinidad, Guyana and the Windward Islands.

'Clive ran the show and was in charge of everything that was happening, though he had some good senior players around him like Viv Richards, Gordon Greenidge, Michael Holding and Joel Garner, players who he knew he could lean on,' said Courtney Walsh, who was a member of the touring party in 1984. 'We all bought in to his philosophies and were in it together. He had the full support of all the players.'

Lloyd was the unofficial head coach at a time when they were not commonplace and would subsequently arrange practice sessions and formulate tactics for matches.

He would perform roles normally attributable to a team manager, choosing room partners with the foresight of always encouraging comradeship and mentoring; maybe a youngster would be partnered with an experienced player, or a Jamaican with a Bajan to promote inter-island mateship. He would be involved with sanctions and team discipline.

Lloyd also worked closely with Australian fitness trainer Dennis Waite to ensure his players were always in the best physical condition.

There was not much that went on around the West Indies team that Lloyd was not central to, and his players knew and appreciated that was how it was. His guidance and philosophies provided the direction and endless drive to keep improving and playing aggressive, positive and, ultimately, winning cricket.

'If the West Indies side around that time was made up differently, it would have caused you to play differently also,' Greenidge said. 'There were so many great things about the side but perhaps the key was having a captain who didn't inhibit his players' natural talent and he encouraged us to express ourselves.

'Clive Lloyd would say, "You go out there and play the way you want to play. Be explosive, be courageous, be forceful." That was great as I don't think a lot of captains would have openly suggested to their players that they go out there and play so freely.

'He never inhibited the players in any way from the way they wanted to play, which was brilliant. That freeness was sometimes our downfall but to have that feeling of self-confidence and knowing you have the backing of the captain to go and get the job done in a way you want to do it was excellent.'

The West Indies needed all those leadership skills and inspiration from Lloyd when they lost the 1983 World Cup Final to India at Lord's. They had gone unbeaten at the 1975 and 1979 World Cups and won both titles, but in '83 they lost to Kapil Dev's India twice, first in the group stage and then the final.

It is said some West Indies players were inconsolable after the match and tears were shed. But what it did do was mark a proverbial line in the sand and Lloyd used it as an opportunity to remind the players they should never again show any mercy or complacency. Not that they intended to lose the final of course, but nonetheless they should have been good enough to chase down those 184 runs required rather than lose by 43 runs.

'There was bitter disappointment because it was a match we should have won fairly easily,' said Winston Davis, who did not play in the final but made his name in the tournament by taking 7-51 against Australia.

'I have thought about the reasons why West Indies faltered that day and the only thing I can come up with is that, without realising it, a bit of complacency crept into our cricket. We bowled well, restricted India, and we should have got those runs with our batting line-up but maybe we were over-confident. Give India their dues, they stuck to the task and got over the line.'

Privately, Lloyd felt let down and accused his players of performing like amateurs. If ever there was a moment to reawaken the giant – the slayers of world cricket – this was it.

The final was supposed to be Lloyd's last game in charge of the West Indies, but the West Indies Cricket Board persuaded him to stay on. Lloyd did not need much coercing as no champion wants to go out on such a loss.

The skipper was glad of the opportunity to avenge the World Cup Final by undertaking a tour of India from October to December of 1983. West Indies won the six-match Test series 3-0 and the five-match one-day series 5-0. Point made.

'We were a better side than India and here we proved it,' Lloyd said. 'We just let ourselves down on the day at Lord's. The fact we went to India and won everything, all eight matches to their none, showed a good professional attitude. We responded in the right way.'

Aside from the cricket, one other aspect that Lloyd observed while in India and which irked him immensely was the adulation that the Indian cricketers were still receiving from various quarters for their World Cup triumph. He saw billboards lauding their efforts everywhere he travelled. Players had been gifted land or cash by the government and, in some cases, luxury apartments or lucrative endorsement contracts.

It was not that Lloyd resented the rewards that came the way of his opponents, some of whom were his friends. It reminded him that when his team won the World Cup they received almost nothing in terms of financial reward. They had to rely on six-month county contracts to top up their earnings.

Lloyd thought such a situation, commercially, had to change in that regard otherwise it would be to the long-term detriment of West Indies cricket. He would be proved right, albeit more than a decade or more later.

Their next main challenge in Test cricket was a home series against Australia, which was won 3-0 after two draws in the first two matches. It was the start of a world record winning streak that numbered 11 matches by the time they won 5-0 in England then wrapped up the five-match series in Australia at the end of the year after winning the first three Tests.

In that home series, the ever-reliable Bajan opening partnership of Gordon Greenidge and Desmond Haynes was functioning well, which took the pressure off the middle order. In the second innings of the first Test in Guyana they registered an unbroken stand of 250, which was only prevented from being greater by the weather.

The West Indies were blessed to have many skilful players in their ranks and the partnership of Greenidge and Haynes was one such positive element to their side that they never took for granted. England, at this time, tried out five different openers on their winter tours to New Zealand and Pakistan.

'You get to know the good points and the bad points of one another's games, and our partnership got to the stage where, with things like running between wickets, we needed very little communication and almost a movement or a gesture was enough,' Greenidge said.

'There were a couple of times when that didn't work out so well but 98 per cent of the time we got the job done.

'Had we not batted together for so long for both Barbados and West Indies perhaps we wouldn't have had that relationship.'

Courtney Walsh made his Test debut on the Australia tour later in the year and although he sat on the sidelines in England in 1984, he was able to further his understanding of what it meant to represent the West Indies.

'After the World Cup the guys seemed closer than ever as team-mates,' Walsh said. 'They were hungrier for success and probably wanted to prove to the world that the World Cup loss wasn't the start of something bad, but the opposite. They were more ambitious than ever.'

By the time the West Indies reached England in May '84, they were back on a roll but still very much feeling the hurt of Lord's almost a year earlier. They carried that defeat around, subconsciously, as a reminder of what can happen when they allowed themselves to feel that things were too easy for them.

Their ruthless, relentless pace attack and their aggressive batsmen could not be matched by any team as long they focused on and conquered their own personal challenges and remained committed to the cause.

Lloyd drove everything in that regard. Two such aspects that his fingerprints were all over, off the field, were team discipline and their attitude to training, especially fielding.

'When we went to practice, like on the Tuesday before a Thursday start to the Test match, we would spend a whole day at the ground,' Lloyd revealed. 'We would bat and bowl in the morning, field in the afternoon and have a nice chat about our plans. We never went back to the hotel until later in the afternoon and would eat lunch at the ground. We were very thorough in our preparations.

'Our fielding was very well drilled. Even all our fast bowlers were gun fielders and capable of fielding in the slips or gully. The only one who didn't field there was Eldine Baptiste.'

Jeffrey Dujon concurred with his former captain's view and remembered many an hour when he and his team-mates would be taking catches or practicing their fielding skills.

'We worked very hard on the slip catching especially,' Dujon said. 'They were really on it, and they had to be sharp in that area with the fast bowlers that we had.

'It created a very competitive situation in practice as the level of intensity that we had in practice itself carried over into matches because practice was conducted as if we were playing in a game. Everybody was competing against each other to be perfect at whatever it was that we were doing, and it showed in our performances. There was no lulling around when it came to our preparation. We operated at a very high level.'

Lloyd was an equally hard taskmaster on discipline. He handed down the message to the youngsters all the way up to his senior players that, if they wanted to stay on top of the world, their standards had to be better than everyone else, and that included off the field. Lloyd was in no way a party-pooper and enjoyed having a drink or attending a sponsor's cocktail party like the next man, but knew the limits of when professionalism would be threatened.

'Discipline in the team was important,' Lloyd said. 'For instance, we would give the guys ten minutes' grace when it came to getting on the bus on time in the morning for practice or a game, but anything after that the guys would shout, "Let the bus roll ..." Many a time did we see guys chasing after the bus with sandwiches in their hands! They would pay a fine into the team kitty.

'Most of the guys were good but there was always someone who tried to get one over on you. I might come back to the hotel after quarter to twelve before the curfew and someone might still be in the nightclub. But it didn't happen too often. The guys realised that if we wanted to be a professional outfit these were the rules we had to follow. But occasionally, because I would put a youngster with a senior roommate, one or two learned the ropes too well!'

It's unlikely Lloyd would have had to have been too strict with his players on the England tour, such was the high standard of their cricket. Off-spinner Roger Harper remembers how excited they were when they arrived in England. A year on from their World Cup low and things had changed significantly.

The squad was in good order, there was strength in depth throughout the line-up with quality waiting to come in should there be an injury. Richie Richardson was ready to open in place of Greenidge or Haynes; Richardson or Gus Logie would come in for any of the middle-order batsmen; the prolific Barbados keeper-batsman Thelston Payne waited patiently in the wings should Dujon become unavailable; while Walsh and Milton Small in the squad or others from outside the squad like Winston Davis or Wayne Daniel were ready to replace any of the pace bowlers. It was all looking very ominous for England.

'The tour of England has always been very special for the West Indies,' Harper said. 'As soon as we arrived we could sense that everyone was keen to do well, especially the guys playing county cricket there. We were determined to ensure the West Indies won the series and won it well.'

Background, England:
A Period of Transition and Struggle

'Those two winter tours that preceded the West Indies'
visit to England in 1984 crystallised the state of the
national team. Sometimes good, sometimes horrid,
maybe glimpses of youthful promise, but usually
inconsistent and often lacking the contributions of
reliable match-winners who got the job done. A
haphazard selection policy didn't help'.

Very early into England's tour of New Zealand in January 1984, in fact just a day after they had arrived in the country and checked into the Sheraton Hotel in Auckland, newspapers carried a story claiming Ian Botham, Allan Lamb and Bob Willis had enjoyed a raucous night in their hotel bar.

'For once the deadly trio were tucked up in bed, jet-lagged, so we knew the story was false,' England's vice-captain on the trip David Gower recalled. 'It turned out the three men who vaguely resembled them were from Wellington and confessed that it was them the story was based on, and they apologised.'

It was during that tour, where England lost the Test series 1-0, that British tabloids became increasingly interested in what the England cricket team were doing off the field, as well as on it. It was later called the *'Sex, Drugs and Rock n roll Tour'*. As is often the case, the media were hungrier for controversial headlines when the team performed badly. And this was such a time. They went on to Pakistan and lost that series, too, also 1-0.

'It had been an era where whatever happened off the field was kind of pushed to one side – until that New Zealand tour,' Gower added. 'It was all based around Beefy (Botham), without wanting to blame him, because of him being the megastar that he was.'

Those two winter tours preceded the West Indies' visit to England in 1984 and crystallised the state of the national team. Sometimes good, sometimes horrid, occasional glimpses of youthful promise, but usually inconsistent and often lacking the contributions of reliable match-winners who got the job done. A haphazard selection policy didn't help.

Further, in the two-year period prior to the 1983/84 winter tours, England had lost the services of some of their best and most experienced cricketers who they had relied upon over the previous decade. Graham Gooch, John Emburey, Geoffrey Boycott, Derek Underwood and Alan Knott were all banned for signing up to the so-called 'rebel' tour of South Africa in 1982.

'By the time we faced the West Indies, it was still a bit of a transitional period, coming away from the nucleus of players who featured in the '81 Ashes and with those guys missing who went to South Africa,' Mike Gatting said. 'Players like Graeme Fowler, Pring (Derek Pringle),

Lamby, Fozzy (Neil Foster), Broady (Chris Broad) and Nick Cook came in with the likes of David Gower, Ian Botham and myself.

'Sometimes you need more experience to help the younger players settle into Test cricket, but we didn't have that chance and therefore too often we were learning the game as opposed to being in the game.'

England's inconsistency was never more evident than during their woeful display at Christchurch in the second Test after they had closed out a tame yet competitive draw in the first Test at Wellington. They collapsed twice at Lancaster Park for 82 and 93, when following on, to lose by an innings and 132 runs inside three days.

While there was some relative inexperience in the team such as opener Fowler, debutant seamer Tony Pigott and young paceman Norman Cowans, there was ample experience and pedigree in the shape of Botham, Gower, captain Willis, wicketkeeper Bob Taylor, and batsmen Gatting and Derek Randall to muster at least a competitive contest. Their meek surrender exposed a soft underbelly that did not bode well only months ahead of a five-Test series with the world-leading West Indies.

'That game in Christchurch was a shocker,' Gower recalled. 'But it wasn't down to shenanigans away from the field or anyone not trying. These things happen to cricket teams. The rot can set in but hopefully that is when someone steps in and says, "Okay, I'll sort this out." But in that particular game, nobody sorted it out.'

To add to Gower's frustration at losing the match so heavily, his mother had flown to Christchurch to visit a cousin and with the hope also of catching some Test cricket. The early finish meant she saw a lot more of her cousin.

'My poignant memory personally,' recalled Gower, 'was facing Richard Hadlee and as the ball left his hand I thought, "I can leave that," and a fraction of a second later I thought, "Oh, no I can't," but by then my gloves were up in the air and as the ball cannoned into my pads there was only going to be one outcome: D.I. Gower ... lbw Hadlee. It looked at first like it was going to miss the stumps by a foot and a half but, as it started to swing, I realised I was in trouble. It was as plumb as you can get so that wasn't a great moment.'

It was New Zealand's maiden Test series win over England, spanning 54 years since they first met. It was, ultimately, a poor result for England but losing to that rapidly developing New Zealand team was not exactly a disgrace or a result to be ashamed of. For England were probably a less settled and competitive Test outfit then than their hosts.

Richard Hadlee and Martin Crowe were genuine world-class players; there was John Wright, a chilled-out guitar-playing nice guy off the field but a gritty, tough competitor on it. Jeremy Coney, another useful combatant who caught well at slip, also scored his share of runs and bowled slow-medium-pacers that infuriated impatient batsmen.

Gower added: 'We'd known for years that New Zealand, as a sporting nation, loved to change the odds. Never to be underestimated even if they never had many superstars.'

A very contrasting tour lay ahead, with a trip to Pakistan on the way home.

England's squad of convivial tourists, who had enjoyed the generous hospitality and leisure options in New Zealand, would fare better on the field in the more unfamiliar, spin-friendly conditions of Pakistan, where leggie Abdul Qadir snared 19 wickets in the series.

Pakistan's two most influential players – Imran Khan and Javed Miandad – were absent in the series, yet England still departed without a confidence-boosting victory that they so desired before taking on the West Indies. But there were shoots of promise.

Not least the form of Gower, who took on the captaincy from Willis for the second and third Tests once Willis had been forced home with a viral infection that he struggled to shift, wholly, for the rest of the English summer. Although neither knew it then, Willis would not lead his country in another Test match and Gower was effectively the captain elect.

It wasn't Gower's Test captaincy debut as he had deputised for Willis against Pakistan at Lord's in 1982, when England lost by ten wickets.

Botham played in the first Test in Karachi but like Willis he also had to return home, injured. That was when he gave his infamous interview and said, 'I wouldn't even send my mother-in-law to Pakistan.'

The comment briefly caused anger amongst Pakistani officials but ultimately for England it was more about ensuring Botham was fit to face the West Indies three months later.

Pakistan won a tight first encounter at Karachi by three wickets when England's batsmen again failed to score sufficient runs to be competitive in the match. Only an impressive 11-wicket haul from left-arm spinner Nick Cook gave England the slightest sniff of a miraculous win on the final day. Pakistan required 65 to win and were nervous at 40/6 as Cook finished with 5-18, but the home side crept over the line.

Gower scored 58 and 57 in the match and was the only England player to register a half-century. Qadir took eight wickets in the match, including Randall twice bowled and Gower lbw, when he initially failed to pick the flipper.

A high-scoring draw at Faisalabad's Iqbal Stadium did not do much for England's chances of winning the series, or even the match, but at least several batsmen were at last able to post some runs on the board and boost morale in that regard. Gower led the way with 152, while Chris Smith (66), Gatting (75), Randall (65), Fowler (57) and all-rounder Vic Marks (83) also passed 50.

Another draw at Lahore gave Pakistan the series but Gower (who made 173 not out) was encouraged by some positive signs as his team almost clinched a most unlikely triumph.

Pakistan required 243 to win and after an opening partnership of 173 between Mohsin Khan and Shoaib Mohammad a home victory seemed academic. Yet they slipped to 199/6 when Norman Cowans' short balls conned the batsmen into finding fielders, to give him 5-42.

'We had to try and make a game of it as we were 1-0 down and you may as well lose 2-0 going for it than holding on to a 1-0 loss,' Gower reflected. 'They started well in their chase, so we experimented with bouncers. They then lost quick wickets and shut up shop. Had they carried on going for it, they may have won, or we may have bowled them out.'

He added: 'Okay, we lost the series, but I wasn't unhappy and thought we made a good fist of things throughout. Personally, I was happy having scored big runs and as captain I felt we came away with some honour due to the way we fought till the end.'

So, the winter tours were done. What did we learn? Mainly, that England were hardly prepared to challenge the world-leading West Indies three months later. Few teams were, in fairness, but England's uncertainty around selection did not bode well. There were lots of questions to be answered before the series.

Would Ian Botham be fit? He was.

Would captain Bob Willis return as skipper? No.

What participation would England's premier, but ageing, fast bowler Willis take in the series? He retired after playing the first three Tests with moderate results.

Would pugnacious middle-order batsman Allan Lamb start the series, having scored just 82 runs in New Zealand at an average of 20, and 78 runs in Pakistan at an average of 15? He did and had the best summer of his career.

Could David Gower retain his incredible form from Pakistan? No, he scored just one fifty in five Tests.

Who would keep, as Bob Taylor's batting struggled badly on tour? Paul Downton came in, after a three-year hiatus.

Norman Cowans and Neil Foster each claimed a five-wicket haul in England's most recent Test in Lahore. Were they, then, certain starters for the first Test v West Indies? No. Cowans only played the fourth Test and Foster featured in just the second Test.

Who would open the innings after four different openers were used on tour (Graeme Fowler, Chris Smith, Chris Tavare and Mike Gatting)? Only Fowler made it from those guys.

Who would be the preferred spinner(s): Vic Marks scored 83, 74 and 55 in the last two Tests of the winter? Nick Cook retained his place, briefly. Marks never played another Test.

In the event, of the XI that played the third and final Test in Pakistan, only four of them featured in more than two Tests against the West Indies, in an era of muddled thinking and over-manoeuvring by the selectors.

'I one hundred per cent felt far from secure in the team even after taking a five-for in Lahore,' Foster said. 'It was probably two or three years before that happened.'

Cowans always felt a similar insecurity as far as national selection was concerned, even after bowling well for his country. 'I don't feel like I ever had a bad tour for England,' Cowans said, 'and I always did myself proud, but still I felt like I was constantly trying to fight my way back into the team.'

Cowans suffered a minor injury after the Pakistan tour, which affected his participation in the West Indies series, but it was always so in his case, even when he was fit.

The captaincy change was less of a surprise as Gower had been primed for the job for two years, though some respected judges from overseas felt he had been thrown to the lions somewhat by the timing of the switch.

Richard Hadlee felt it was a good decision to promote Gower but suggested he needed the West Indies series to be looked upon almost like a free pass, given this was a long-term move. 'It'll be two to three years, I reckon, before England becomes a dominant force again, and Gower needs that period to learn the art of captaincy and to mould a youthful team into something that can compete,' Hadlee commented. 'Playing your first series against the West Indies is about the toughest baptism you could have – a nightmare for any captain.'

For Gower himself, he knew he had been Willis's understudy and the promotion to captain of England did not come as a shock when the decision was officially made on 23 May. Gower had a reputation as someone who understood the game well and would therefore improve England tactically.

John Woodcock wrote in *The Times* that Gower was the best batsman to lead England since then chairman of selectors, Peter May. He also wrote that some selectors considered Gower 'too casual or modern for their liking' and he had little experience of captaincy.

Willis was a popular captain among team-mates but was not seen as an inspirational game-changer. When focused and 'psyched-up' about his own bowling, it wasn't unusual to have wicketkeeper Bob Taylor, ex-captain Botham and vice-captain Gower all fiddling with field placings, at different times. There was a void as far as a central figure of authority went. Gower was seen as someone who could fill that vacuum.

'The small print was that my first challenge would be against the best team in the world, arguably the strongest side of all time,' Gower reflected. 'So, you have this conversation between your public self and your private self. Your public self is saying, "Okay, they are a good side but they're only human. If we have a bit of luck and play well, we will at least compete. If we're *really* lucky, we might even win something." Then your private self is saying, "How the fuck do we beat these guys?" You look down their batting side and then look at their bowling attack and then you look at your own team and think, "Okay, well, we'll give it a go." The challenge was an immense one.'

Missing Rebels and Surplus Talent

'The bottom line: due to three-year bans on the so-called "rebels" who toured South Africa in 1981/82, England missed several players for this Test series who would certainly have made a positive difference to the contest. Whether that would have affected the 5-0 outcome will never be known.

'Conversely, the West Indies were also affected by bans on their own players. But, quite simply, they didn't need them, or miss them. In fact, they had such a wealth of talent to select from that their biggest problem was who to leave out.'

The many county matches that existed on an overseas tour in days gone by were generally there to provide practice in English conditions. Key players either sat out or casually looked at the games to find form; the youngsters gained exposure and experience.

There was little to gain from a home viewpoint other than the chance to measure oneself against internationals, in fact the very best when the West Indians were in town. Generally, there was not much scope to pique interest, but every now and then there would be a performance that demanded attention.

Such an example stood out at Chelmsford in late June, sandwiched between the first and second Tests after England's batsmen had been hammered by West Indian pace at Edgbaston, culminating in an innings defeat.

Graham Gooch plundered 101 for Essex and it was enough to spark contemplation at how stronger England would have been with him involved in the Test series, rather than seeing out the third and final year of his ban for touring South Africa with England's 'rebels' in 1981/82. Essex named a strong team for that match including internationals such as Keith Fletcher, Ken McEwan, young England all-rounder Derek Pringle and several first-team regulars, yet no other batsman reached 40 in their first innings of 267/9 declared. It was the Gooch Show.

Okay, there was no Malcolm Marshall or Michael Holding, but there was still Joel Garner, an up-and-coming Courtney Walsh, Milton Small, who played at Lord's, and the off-spinner Roger Harper, who picked up many important Test wickets that summer.

It was not as though Gooch was untried, after all, for his pedigree was already proven against the West Indies so this innings merely reminded the England selectors how badly he was missed.

Gooch was by then a far cry from the rookie who perished to the innocuous off-spin of Collis King and the gentle medium pace of Clive Lloyd in a tour match for Essex on West Indies' tour in 1976. He had gritted his way to a brilliant 123 at Lord's in the 1980 Test series when facing Andy Roberts, Holding, Garner and Colin Croft; added 83 at The Oval where Marshall had come in for Roberts; and then in the subsequent return series in 1980/81 he made 83 in Antigua and a determined 153 in Jamaica.

'Gooch had such a good track record against the West Indies that he would have been the obvious one to have played in the 1984 series from the rebel squad,' said Dennis Amiss, who was a team-mate on that controversial South African trip. 'Goochie became one of the best ever for England.' The Guyanese spinner Harper agreed with Amiss, adding that England 'definitely missed a player of his quality and fortitude'.

The rebel tour squad mainly consisted of players who were nearing the end of their careers, such as Amiss, Alan Knott, Geoffrey Boycott and Derek Underwood. That's why Gooch's inclusion in that squad created surprise and disappointment from an England perspective.

Gooch, 28 when he toured South Africa, claimed to have been bored by cricket at the time and needed an exciting challenge, which he felt was provided by that opportunity. Most in the squad were honest enough to acknowledge their decisions were financially motivated, at a time when county salaries were modest.

Gooch's Essex team-mate Pringle knew better than most how England suffered for the absence of one of their best batsmen against pace bowling.

'Gooch was an enormous loss – he would have played for sure,' Pringle said. 'Keith Fletcher used to say if the ball was bouncing above the knee-roll, Goochie was the best batsman in England to face it. Obviously against the West Indies that was often the case as they liked to bang it in.' Gooch's fellow 1981 Ashes winner Mike Gatting concurred with Pringle, adding: 'An opening batsman of the calibre of Graham Gooch was always very useful against a side like the West Indies.'

If Gooch was the one obvious miss for England, there were more who would certainly have come into contention if not being an obvious starter, such as batting all-rounder Peter Willey and opener Wayne Larkins. Middlesex off-spinner John Emburey was another who many considered a significant loss because of the South Africa ban.

Emburey would have been a reliable, economical spinner in the 1984 series, according to his Middlesex team-mate Gatting, as well as being a decent batsman down the order and a good catcher. Statistically, though, the figures dispute this argument for 'Embers' averaged over 40 with the ball in his seven Tests against the West Indies at home and eight away.

Nonetheless, Pringle's view that Emburey was England's best spinner was echoed by most of the England players of the day.

One spin bowler whose numbers never seemed to decline, however, no matter how old he became, was Underwood. The argument to pick 'Deadly' in the '84 series did not seem so obvious to those England players who were canvassed, though once they reflected on his form for Kent during his ban most admitted they would have found it difficult to oppose his inclusion.

Underwood's 39th birthday came just days prior to the Test series, though he was still young enough to be considered a worthy, experienced option. Especially as England reverted to Pat 'Percy' Pocock for the final two Tests, demonstrating how the selectors were not biased by age as Pocock was only a year younger than Underwood.

Slow left-armer Underwood, who took 297 wickets in his 86 Tests, snared a national high of 105 wickets in the County Championship in 1983 at an average of 19.27, just ahead of Emburey's 96 and Norman Gifford's 99. He retired at the end of the 1986 county season.

Paul Downton played all five Tests against Clive Lloyd's men in 1984 and kept to the veteran spinner when starting out as a rookie county pro in 1977. He considered it 'a very good question' as to whether Underwood would still have been a Test player in '84.

'He was a phenomenon and still a very effective bowler in his later years,' Downton commented. 'The fact the selectors recalled Pat Pocock suggests age would not have been a problem. That Geoff Miller, Nick Cook and Pocock all played in the series shows how we were struggling to find a regular spinner.'

Andy Lloyd, who made his Test debut that summer, was another to trumpet Underwood's obvious inclusion against the West Indies had he not been banned. Lloyd regarded 'Deadly' as 'an unbelievable bowler' who got better with age.

'My old team-mate Norman Gifford was a wonderful bowler too, and better than those other spinners who played in the series by a street,' Lloyd said. 'The only reason Giff didn't play more (than his 15 Tests) for England was the presence of Derek Underwood.'

Amiss suggested his England and Warwickshire colleague Chris Old might also have come into contention for a seam bowling position that summer, because of his similarity to Stuart Broad of the modern day. But he was ultimately another to suffer for his rebel tour ban.

Underwood's Kent team-mate and pace bowler Graham Dilley was not banned that summer but injured. Physical ailments limited 'Picca' to just one Test in three years between July 1983 and June 1986 – he featured in the second Test against Pakistan at Faisalabad in 1984.

Many players felt he would have been another to have made a positive difference against the West Indies. England had the tourists in trouble on several occasions but struggled to access the firepower required to finish them off. 'Dilley was the best fast bowler we had after Bob,' Pringle said, 'but for some curious reason he never quite believed in himself.'

Skipper David Gower also admitted that Dilley's absence was a blow, as he had demonstrated previously what he was capable of.

'We missed him, yes,' Gower acknowledged. 'Graham, bless him, had genuine pace and with Bob at the end of his career, we were short of absolute firepower. On our tour of the Caribbean in '81 he hurried the best and even had Viv hopping. The pitches in '84, though, were probably too flat but still it would have been nice to have had Dil available to us.'

Let us allow ourselves some playful indulgence – or 'fantasy cricket' – and second-guess what the England team might have been in 1984 had it not been for the rebel tour bans and injuries. As you will see the third seamer's position after Botham and Dilley is difficult as an ageing Willis might not have been such an automatic pick with the presence of Dilley.

Boycott may justifiably claim superiority over Fowler then, having amassed 1,941 County Championship runs in 1983 at 55.45, and then 1,567 runs at 62.68 in 1984. Impressive numbers indeed in his early forties. How about this line-up ...

England: Gooch; Fowler; Gower; Lamb; Gatting; Botham; Downton; Emburey; (then either Pringle/Willis/ Allott/Ellison/Cowans/Foster/Old); Dilley; Underwood.

Ultimately, even with Gooch, Emburey, Dilley and Underwood in the ranks, no England player from then was bold enough to suggest their inclusions would have altered West Indian dominance that summer. Maybe it could have been 4-1?

'I'm sure Graham, and the other guys, would have made us stronger but I'm not so sure the final equation would have changed too much,' Foster concluded. 'The fact Goochie scored a hundred (129 not out) in '86 when we won a one-day international in the Caribbean – our only win there – suggests Goochie would certainly have made a big difference. But who's to say by how much?'

Pringle shared Foster's pragmatism. 'Even if we had Goochie, Embers and Dilley, I'm not sure it would have made much difference. They were that good. Maybe we would have drawn at Lord's.'

As for the West Indies, there were far fewer selection headaches, if any at all ...

It's conjecture of course, but it is possible that the West Indies were so strong in that era, from the mid-70s to the late 80s, that they could have fielded a second string XI and still beaten any Test team in the world. Maybe not 5-0 but there was so much high-class talent from the Caribbean that their greatest problem was excess waste.

By the time of the '84 England tour, they had experienced their own share of disruption from South African rebel tours between 1982 and 1984. It just didn't affect them from a playing standpoint, but more culturally as those who toured South Africa were handed life bans and faced long-term vilification.

The higher-profile names who went to South Africa were Lawrence Rowe, a brilliant stroke maker who famously scored a century and double century on Test debut, Alvin Kallicharran, another batsman with a wealth of Test experience behind him, and the fiery fast bowler Colin Croft, whose 8-29 in his second Test remains West Indies' second-best analysis in a Test innings.

The truth is though, despite the injustices of selection, Kallicharran and Rowe hadn't played a Test for four years so had barely been missed by a dominant West Indies. 'I don't think any of them would have made our team,' Lloyd said. 'We had to look to the future. Gomes was ahead of Kallicharran by then.'

Equally, while Croft was still young enough at 31 to continue his Test career there was not exactly a demand for his recall with the wealth of pace bowlers in the system.

'It was already a very settled situation in the team,' Jeffrey Dujon commented. 'If Crofty had been fit and had stayed around I'm not sure he would have been around the team for long anyway given what we had coming in the pace-bowling department. We were very competently covered in his position.'

The West Indies were strong enough to even allow Andy Roberts to slip into international retirement when aged only 33 and he was good enough to take 33 wickets at 23 in eight matches for Leicestershire in '84.

'There are so many things you try to do right as a captain and in the case of Andy I wanted him to leave on his own terms as opposed to being left out because he was a legend and deserved more than that,' Lloyd said. 'He'd had one or two injuries, and we were strong in that department with Malcolm, Joel, Mikey, Eldine and Winston Davis, who was coming through. I'm sure Andy could still have done a good job, but we were well off for fast bowlers then.'

The two disappointing, or even sad, cases from their rebel squad were those of young all-rounder Franklyn Stephenson and fast bowler Ezra Moseley. Aged 25 and 26 respectively they could well have had lengthy Test careers but for their decisions to accept lucrative offers from South Africa.

Moseley was the only rebel to play for the West Indies again once the bans were lifted in 1989. He possessed a deceptive pace uncomfortable enough to break Graham Gooch's hand in Trinidad in 1990. Stephenson, meantime, compensated the loss of an international career by becoming a sought-after overseas player in South Africa, Australia and England, notably for Nottinghamshire, where he perfected a slower ball yorker.

There will always be two names, though, whose short West Indies careers stand out from the rest. Fast bowlers Sylvester Clarke and Wayne Daniel would almost certainly have played over 50 Test matches each for any other nation, such was their wicket-taking quality.

Daniel played just ten Tests between 1976 and 1984 and would have been in his prime in 1984 at 28. Instead, he was a popular long-term overseas player at Middlesex where he played an integral role in their trophy-laden success, winning three County Championship titles, three Gillette Cups/NatWest Trophies and two Benson & Hedges Cups.

'The West Indies had so many great fast bowlers then and Wayne was just unlucky to be born at that time when opportunities to play for the West Indies were less than they might have been at a different time,' said his new-ball partner at Middlesex, Norman Cowans.

'It has been the same for other players through the years. Look at Bob Taylor – he was a brilliant wicketkeeper but because of the time he played he had to live in Alan Knott's shadow for so long. It was the same for Wayne. "Diamond" was a great fast bowler and had he been born 20 years later he would have been an automatic choice, as most of the West Indies' quicks born in more recent times aren't good enough to lace Wayne's boots. He only knew one way to bowl and that was fast.

'Fortunately for us, Middlesex had the best out of him rather than West Indies and he was a huge part of our success in that time. Wayne was a wholehearted bowler who made things happen. If we were struggling for a wicket, so often Gatt would throw the ball to Wayne and ask him to grab us a wicket and he usually did.'

Clarke, who would have been 29 in 1984, elected to tour South Africa with the rebels having become frustrated by his lack of international opportunities. He is spoken of in South Africa and especially England, where he played over a nine-year period for Surrey, with such reverence and retrospective fear it's unfathomable that he also played so few Tests – just 11.

'He was another victim of the strength we had in our fast-bowling department,' Lloyd said. 'But boy, he was quick. Whenever I faced him at The Oval or in Barbados, there always seemed to be someone on the sidelines shouting to him, "Sylvester man, this the guy who keeping you out of the West Indies!" So, I had to face Clarkey at his quickest.'

Whereas Daniel ran in with the enthusiasm and transparent aggression of a fast bowler seemingly intent on knocking the batsman's head off, Clarke's threat was much more subtle but no less hostile. In fact, he is usually the one bowler that county batsmen from the 1980s recall most fearfully.

'I was proud to score a good hundred against him once, but he was a nightmare to bat against,' said Andy Lloyd. 'He was a very aggressive and angry bowler.'

Clarke's reputation in his homeland was equally respectful. When he tragically died aged just 44 in 1999, there was an outpouring of grief, shock, but also of regret that we didn't see more of him for the West Indies. In his penultimate match against Pakistan at Multan, he reacted to being pelted with fruit while fielding on the boundary by tossing a (boundary) house brick into the crowd. That also didn't aid his Test prospects.

'I have two words to describe Sylvester's bowling,' said Dujon. 'Extremely dangerous. His first four overs with the new ball, wow. He was awkward because he just ran through the crease with a big, strong upper body and tended to bowl quite short, a lot.'

Pat Pocock revealed that he heard numerous horror stories from batsmen at other counties of how they hated to face his Surrey team-mate.

'When we were in India on the 1984/85 tour there wasn't lots to do off the field and in the more remote areas we found ourselves talking cricket an awful lot,' Pocock recalled. 'One of the sources of conversation that repeatedly came up was how much batsmen on the county circuit genuinely feared playing against Sylvester. They didn't enjoy him at all.'

Daniel and Clarke were two of the higher-profile victims of the West Indies talent pool at that time, but they were far from alone. Winston Davis, Tony Gray, Carlisle Best, Clyde Butts, Tony Merrick, Ralston Otto, Rangy Nanan, Ganesh Mahabir ... there were plenty. Even Eldine Baptiste, who had played ten, won ten by the conclusion of the 1984 series, didn't play again for six years!

A Schedule from Hell

'It was quite taxing and frenetic for a lot of us who were not used to playing so much cricket, especially without breaks in between. But we enjoyed the opportunities to learn' – Roger Harper

The 1984 West Indies Tour of the British Isles, itinerary: *(scheduled days for cricket)*

Saturday 19 May	v Worcestershire, Worcester (3-day game)
Sunday 20 May	v Worcestershire, Worcester
Monday 21 May	v Worcestershire, Worcester
Tuesday 22 May	REST/TRAVEL DAY
Wednesday 23 May	v Somerset, Taunton (3-day game)
Thursday 24 May	v Somerset, Taunton
Friday 25 May	v Somerset, Taunton
Saturday 26 May	v Glamorgan, Swansea (3-day game)
Sunday 27 May	v Glamorgan, Swansea
Monday 28 May	v Glamorgan, Swansea
Tuesday 29 May	v Lancashire, Liverpool (55-over game)
Wednesday 30 May	REST/TRAVEL DAY
Thursday 31 May	v England, Manchester (1st One-Day International)
Friday 1 June	REST/TRAVEL DAY
Saturday 2 June	v England, Nottingham (2nd One-Day International)
Sunday 3 June	REST/TRAVEL DAY
Monday 4 June	v England, Lord's, London (3rd One-Day International)

Tuesday 5 June	REST/TRAVEL DAY
Wednesday 6 June	v Lavinia, Duchess of Norfolk's XI, Arundel (50-over game)
Thursday 7 June	v Oxford/Cambridge Universities, Oxford (2-day game)
Friday 8 June	v Oxford/Cambridge Universities, Oxford
Saturday 9 June	v Northamptonshire, Bletchley (3-day game)
Sunday 10 June	v Northamptonshire, Bletchley
Monday 11 June	v Northamptonshire, Bletchley
Tuesday 12 June	REST/TRAVEL DAY
Wednesday 13 June	REST/TRAVEL DAY
Thursday 14 June	v England, Birmingham (1st Test)
Friday 15 June	v England, Birmingham
Saturday 16 June	v England, Birmingham
Sunday 17 June	REST DAY
Monday 18 June	v England, Birmingham
Tuesday 19 June	v England, Birmingham
Wednesday 20 June	REST/TRAVEL DAY
Thursday 21 June	v Ireland, Dublin (2-day game)
Friday 22 June	v Ireland, Dublin
Saturday 23 June	v Essex, Chelmsford (3-day game)
Sunday 24 June	v Essex, Chelmsford
Monday 25 June	v Essex, Chelmsford
Tuesday 26 June	REST/TRAVEL DAY
Wednesday 27 June	REST/TRAVEL DAY
Thursday 28 June	v England, Lord's, London (2nd Test)
Friday 29 June	v England, Lord's, London
Saturday 30 June	v England, Lord's, London
Sunday 1 July	REST DAY
Monday 2 July	v England, Lord's, London
Tuesday 3 July	v England, Lord's, London
Wednesday 4 July	REST/TRAVEL DAY
Thursday 5 July	v League Cricket Conference, Colwyn Bay (2-day game)
Friday 6 July	v League Cricket Conference, Colwyn Bay
Saturday 7 July	v Leicestershire, Leicester (3-day game)
Sunday 8 July	v Leicestershire, Leicester
Monday 9 July	v Leicestershire, Leicester

Tuesday 10 July	REST/TRAVEL DAY
Wednesday 11 July	REST/TRAVEL DAY
Thursday 12 July	v England, Leeds (3rd Test)
Friday 13 July	v England, Leeds
Saturday 14 July	v England, Leeds
Sunday 15 July	REST DAY
Monday 16 July	v England, Leeds
Tuesday 17 July	v England, Leeds
Wednesday 18 July	REST/TRAVEL DAY
Thursday 19 July	v Minor Counties, West Bromwich (2-day game)
Friday 20 July	v Minor Counties, West Bromwich
Saturday 21 July	v Derbyshire, Derby (3-day game)
Sunday 22 July	v Derbyshire, Derby
Monday 23 July	v Derbyshire, Derby
Tuesday 24 July	v Lancashire, Southport (40-over match)
Wednesday 25 July	REST/TRAVEL DAY
Thursday 26 July	v England, Manchester (4th Test)
Friday 27 July	v England, Manchester
Saturday 28 July	v England, Manchester
Sunday 29 July	REST DAY
Monday 30 July	v England, Manchester
Tuesday 31 July	v England, Manchester
Wednesday 1 August	v Nottinghamshire, Nottingham (3-day game)
Thursday 2 August	v Nottinghamshire, Nottingham
Friday 3 August	v Nottinghamshire, Nottingham
Saturday 4 August	v Middlesex, Lord's, London (3-day game)
Sunday 5 August	v Middlesex, Lord's, London
Monday 6 August	v Middlesex, Lord's, London
Tuesday 7 August	REST/TRAVEL DAY
Wednesday 8 August	REST/TRAVEL DAY
Thursday 9 August	v England, The Oval, London (5th Test)
Friday 10 August	v England, The Oval, London
Saturday 11 August	v England, The Oval, London
Sunday 12 August	REST DAY
Monday 13 August	v England, The Oval, London
Tuesday 14 August	v England, The Oval, London
Wednesday 15 August	REST/TRAVEL DAY

Thursday 16 August v Kent, Gillingham (40-over game/Benefit
for Bob Woolmer)
Friday 17 August   v Somerset, Taunton (50-over game/Benefit
for Jock McCoombe)
Saturday 18 August Official End of Tour

If a touring team of the current day was expected to commit
to West Indies' schedule of 1984, they might just vote to
boycott, while their medical team would rub their eyes in
disbelief.

Clive Lloyd's men were falling out of one match into
another without any rest days at times. Back-to-back
three-day games with Somerset and Glamorgan at the
start of the tour were followed by a one-day match against
Lancashire, just prior to the Texaco Trophy one-day series.
The presence of Australian fitness trainer Dennis Waite
was much needed, to keep their overworked players on the
field and off the treatment table.

To Lloyd and his team-mates, though, it was business
as usual and there were no complaints from the players.

'The upside was that the travel wasn't too far, game to
game, we had a nice bus, and we were able to rotate the
squad,' Lloyd said. 'But yes, the games did come thick
and fast, but it was an opportunity to blood youngsters
and see what they could do, which doesn't tend to happen
as much now.

'We agreed a tour fee with our board beforehand,
which off memory was $10,000 US a man. On top of that
I would get an extra allowance for being captain and Viv
probably got more for being vice-captain, but all prize
money and everything else was shared equally. In those

days our board was paid well by the host country for such a tour and enjoyed the fruits of our labour. Nowadays we have come the full circle because the West Indies get a fraction of what the bigger countries like India, Australia and England get.'

Touring teams became accustomed to such frenetic itineraries in England, but this one seemed to be as demanding as any, bordering on physically dangerous. Although the team management did their best to rotate selection for the games outside of the international matches, it was still a lot of cricket; especially for the fast bowlers, who required sufficient rest away from the grander challenges.

Not that the players complained as it was just the norm that they had become accustomed to. The West Indies' three-and-a-half-month tour of England in 1980 wasn't much different although it had five more official days off than the tour of '84.

'The 1984 tour schedule felt no different to previous tours,' Michael Holding said. 'Touring teams used to play every county team and some teams twice during a UK tour, so it was similar to being in a county team.'

The biggest winners were the squad players who were not Test regulars or sure of their place. Deputy wicketkeeper Thelston Payne, back-up batsmen Richie Richardson and Gus Logie and reserve pace bowlers Milton Small and Courtney Walsh enjoyed their game time, as did Roger Harper, Eldine Baptiste and late call-up Winston Davis, none of whom were sure of their Test places.

Captain Lloyd, vice-captain Viv Richards, deputy vice-captain Gordon Greenidge, Michael Holding, Malcolm Marshall, Joel Garner, Desmond Haynes, wicketkeeper Jeff Dujon, and probably Larry Gomes were shoo-ins for the Test matches. That left room for just two positions where there might be some competition for places. In the event, Baptiste and Harper played all five Tests.

'It was a long tour where we played against most of the counties and the opportunity was there for the youngsters to gain experience in those conditions,' Harper said. 'The core of the team was already established, and the youngsters were merely expected to give a good account of themselves. They were there mainly as back-up and to blossom from whatever chances they had.

'The experienced guys did most of the heavy lifting. It was a tremendous opportunity for the younger guys to learn from the senior players, especially about the culture of the team. Besides, our schedule was just like how county cricket was set up. I played county cricket the following year and remember playing something like 23 days on the trot, it was non-stop.

'It was quite taxing and frenetic for a lot of us who were not used to playing so much cricket, especially without breaks in between. But it was a new experience that I enjoyed.'

Someone like Trinidad & Tobago middle-order batsman Gus Logie would be the perfect example of a player who profited from the schedule, as he was able to play eight first-class games outside of the internationals and plundered 585 runs at an average of 73.12.

By that stage Logie was aged 23 and had already played nine Tests but had yet to establish himself. The tour was another chance to push his claims. Similarly, Courtney Walsh had been in and around the squad but was yet to make his Test debut. He was grateful of the added exposure to the West Indies team.

'The culture was excellent, it was like a family unit, everyone was in it together,' Walsh reminisced. 'Even if some guys didn't get along outside of cricket, nobody would have known because of how professional they were. It was a tremendous learning curve for me to be part of it. I was blessed to be in the same dressing room with these greats, and then in the same team. To share the field with them was a dream come true.'

The interesting aspect to this is that this was a normal working rota for England's players, too.

They would flip-flop from county game to county game to England match, without much of a rest or time for quality practice or planning meetings. That was county cricket in the 1980s. It isn't massively different today for county players, but a significant improvement has been felt by England's players courtesy of the implementation of the central contract scheme in 2000, whereby their schedules are now governed by the cricket board and not their county.

In 1984, though, the notion of Gower missing Leicestershire's tourist match against the Windies was unheard of as he was club captain – and they were paying his wages. The endless cricket could be quite ridiculous at times.

In between the first and second Tests, Gower and Allan Lamb participated in the Tilcon Trophy, which was barely a second-tier competition. Maybe it was slightly ahead of a second XI tournament but only just. They would likely have preferred a break for a few days but that was wishful thinking.

Leicestershire won the Tilcon Trophy, beating Lamb's Northamptonshire in the final at Harrogate.

'That's how it was; everyone was playing full-on. It was bonkers,' Gower recalled with a smile. 'When central contracts finally came in, these situations were slowly eradicated. Games like these in the Tilcon Trophy were light relief in a way. They were pretty much exhibition games. You're staying in a B&B and playing on a club ground basically, it's hilarious. Imagine saying to Ben Stokes now, how do you fancy playing the Tilcon Trophy after the Lord's Test? We didn't question it then, you just played them.'

The competition, which ran between 1976 and 1998, was also known by various sponsors' names as the Harrogate Festival Trophy, Tetley Bitter Trophy and the Costcutter Cup.

What was more routine was going from a late finish in a County Championship match on a Tuesday, to a Test match on a Wednesday, ready to start next day.

Gower, Lamb and all their England colleagues left an energy-sapping Test match at Lord's against the West Indies in '84 on the Tuesday evening and were driving cross-country to be ready to play a 60-over-a-side one-day match in the NatWest Trophy the following morning.

Imagine how excited Ian Botham would have been to be in Hertfordshire, opening the bowling to a couple of club players, the morning after bowling 20 overs at an inspired Gordon Greenidge the day before! The only consolation for him was the relatively short drive from north London to St Albans, where the game was played.

Gower had to drive to Swindon to play Wiltshire, Mike Gatting and Paul Downton departed for Jesmond in the North East, similarly Lamb had to drive for four hours to play Durham at Darlington, while Bob Willis was pounding in again at Edgbaston against Oxfordshire.

'That was knackering,' Lamb acknowledged, 'and it would have been harder on the bowlers, but in those days we drove all over the bloody place all the time.'

Botham, Willis, Gatting and Gower were all captains at their respective counties so they would have felt the mental strain also, with having to get to grips with domestic matters. Gower was grateful for the support of his dependable vice-captain Peter Willey.

'The problem was as much for the county as me,' Gower explained. 'You come back to the club from a Test match and although the scorebook might say you haven't done much, you're still drained and have lost a tough game.

'You need to pick yourself up mentally and catch up on what has been going on with the club after being away from things for a week. They might have played two Championship games and a Sunday game while you've been away.

'You need good advice on what's been going on and Pete was great like that. I might have finished a Test match on the Tuesday night and by Wednesday morning you're about to start another Championship match thinking, "Right, who's here, who's been doing what?"

'It was only a good thing in the way you had no time to dwell on the defeat, in this case to the West Indies. It was all non-negotiable and you knew you had to pick yourself up very quickly and get on with things by going back to your county and scoring runs, in my case, whether it's at Wiltshire in the NatWest or wherever.

'Not only was the cricket relentless, but the schedule was also relentless. When you're losing a Test series like we were it's a bloody tough ask to continually keep trying to pick yourself up and go and play for your county.'

Over the years, we have seen touring teams at their leisure, enjoying themselves during downtime in England, whether it was the Pakistan team at Alton Towers theme park in 2001, the Australia squad visiting the greyhound races in Birmingham in 2005 through Ricky Ponting's links to that sport, while various players have attended Wimbledon, and Steve Waugh's tour squad in 2001 even visited Gallipoli in Turkey en route to England.

'I was always interested in horse racing so that would have consumed some hours on tour,' Michael Holding said. 'I don't think I had time to actually go to a racetrack while on tour in England, but I followed the races closely.'

Holding's fellow Jamaican Jeff Dujon agreed that players had the chance to do their own thing in 1984, but felt the schedule was so demanding that nobody did anything too adventurous.

'Off the field everyone tended to go their own way,' Dujon recalled. 'You spend so much time together that sometimes you don't want to do anything or see any of your team-mates, so you might just go out for lunch or dinner with friends.

'Every player had their own way of relaxing and doing what they felt they needed to do to rest or unwind. But I don't remember us doing anything all together. And the cricket came so thick and fast on that tour that we never had much free time anyway. I don't remember getting too many games off.'

Courtney Walsh, who became Holding's new roommate as Andy Roberts was no longer travelling with the team, ultimately saw the tour as a significant education in his cricket journey, despite the frustrations at merely being a back-up player taking on the counties.

'I was disappointed not to play any Test cricket on that tour, but I was a rookie and my role was to play the side games and just make sure I learnt from the senior guys as much as I could,' said Walsh. 'To watch the quality of cricket they played, the never-say-die attitude they showed, the confidence they had to always get the job done was something extra special.'

Results:

v Worcestershire	Match drawn
v Somerset	West Indians won by an innings and 101 runs
v Glamorgan	West Indians won by an innings and 226 runs
v Lancashire	West Indians won by 56 runs
v England, 1st One-Day Int.	West Indies won by 104 runs
v England, 2nd One-Day Int.	England won by 3 wickets
v England, 3rd One-Day Int.	West Indies won by 8 wickets
v Lavinia, Duchess of Norfolk's XI	West Indians won by 64 runs
v Oxford/Cambridge Universities	Match drawn
v Northamptonshire	Match drawn
v England, 1st Test	West Indies won by an innings and 180 runs
v Ireland	Match drawn
v Essex	Match drawn
v England, 2nd Test	West Indies won by 9 wickets
v League Cricket Conference	Match drawn
v Leicestershire	Match drawn
v England, 3rd Test	West Indies won by 8 wickets
v Minor Counties	Match drawn
v Derbyshire	West Indians won by an innings and 169 runs
v Lancashire	West Indians won by 17 runs
v England, 4th Test	West Indies won by an innings and 64 runs
v Nottinghamshire	Match drawn
v Middlesex	Match drawn
v England, 5th Test	West Indies won by 172 runs
v Kent	West Indians won *(benefit match)*
v Somerset	Somerset won *(benefit match)*

Viv's Masterclass Sets the Tone

'Viv was the only one who could have played that innings. It wasn't pleasant to be on the receiving end as a bowler, but in hindsight I'm strangely proud to have been a part of it as it was such an historic innings.' – Neil Foster

If ever there was a microcosm of the summer between these two teams it came at Old Trafford in the first one-day international. England threatened to win by taking a clump of West Indian wickets very quickly, before the tourists rallied and eventually strolled towards an overwhelming victory.

It was one of the most extreme examples of how and why a world champion team is just that: by demonstrating resilience, belief, tenacity, but more than anything in this match possessing players who are simply mercurial. Or geniuses. That was, after all, Viv Richards personified. Gifted beyond reasonable comprehension.

For England to reduce the West Indies to 102/7, there seemed only one likely winner and it wasn't the West Indies. How, then, did they end up posting 272/9 in their 55 overs? Quite simply because Richards played the innings of his life – though there were a few of those – scoring 189 not out.

A once-buoyant England were left shell-shocked, and it was no surprise when they capitulated to 168 all out in reply. To say the 104-run win was unusual would be an understatement; it was based on a performance that most careers are never likely to come close to seeing.

Richards added 106 for the ninth wicket with Michael Holding, who faced just 27 balls for his 12 not out, during an hour at the crease in which he did his best to stay with his senior batsman but in fact he more likely was in awe for much of the time. He wasn't alone.

David Gower: 'The one thing I can say about that innings is we had a great view of a very special knock. Whatever we tried, it just went in the opposite direction for six. If we could have got Mikey out quickly it would have been a very close, exciting game. But Viv had other ideas.'

Graeme Fowler: 'We walked off stunned. As we sat down in the dressing room, no one spoke. Then Beefy said simply, "Smokey, you bastard."'

Neil Foster: 'Viv was the only one who could have played that innings. It wasn't pleasant to be on the receiving end as a bowler, but in hindsight I'm strangely proud to have been a part of it as it was such an historic innings. It felt too raw at the time to feel that way then, but you still knew and appreciated that something special had happened.'

Geoff Miller: 'I was fielding at long-on, and the ball just kept disappearing over my head towards the railway line. They were monster hits. Viv was a genius. He's the one guy from my generation who I would be certain could excel in the modern game with Twenty20 and with the emphasis more tilted towards attack.'

Derek Pringle: 'It was extraordinary. I was almost awestruck even though I was in the middle of it.'

Mike Gatting: 'I had never seen an innings like it. Even now I still say to people that was the best innings I ever saw. What he did, to take the West Indies from where they were to 272, was quite unbelievable from an individual. I'll never forget some of those strokes, like coming down the wicket and whacking Bob Willis over cover. It was very special.'

Jeffrey Dujon: 'We were in a bit of trouble, and I never expected we would end up getting to where we did. It just highlighted how good a player he was. It was not only his obvious talent but the character that he showed. He seemed to have it all worked out.'

Andy Lloyd: 'It was my first game for England. It was an extraordinary innings. Gower was obviously aware of trying to get Mikey Holding on strike and he did all he could to do that, but Viv's rotation, running between wickets and his hitting was sensational.'

If Richards' score and the way he went about making those runs wasn't phenomenal enough, his expression of confidence in what he told his team-mates in the dressing room at the lunch break on that day in May was another thing.

West Indies were teetering on 11/2 when Richards went out to bat and things were much worse at lunch.

An upbeat, pumped-up Richards walked in to greet his gloomy team.

'The mood was very sombre in our dressing room after we had lost those early wickets,' Roger Harper remembered. 'Viv was batting with Eldine Baptiste and he came in at the lunch break, looked around and said, "What's the matter with you guys? Why are you so glum? Don't worry, I'm going to take them apart." Those were his exact words. He said to Baptiste, "You just stay with me. Today is Viv Richards' Day." It was one of those days where every ball seemed to hit the middle of his bat.'

Baptiste had a similar recollection and was pleased to witness his fellow Antiguan in such a buoyant and optimistic mindset. That positivity soon rubbed off on him once they resumed the innings after lunch.

'I was facing Geoff Miller to a slip, a short leg and a silly point,' Baptiste recalled. 'The great man wandered down to me and said, "You're better than that. You must not let him bowl to you with that field." I said, "But I'm just sticking around for you." He said, "Yes, I know that. But you're better that that (nodding at the field placings). You play your natural game. If it's there to be hit, you hit it." I was more confident after that pep-talk, and we put on 59.

'He was insistent that I played in a positive way. He told me to commit to the shot and not have any doubts. He carried on with Mikey once I was out and it was the most outstanding innings I had ever seen. I had never seen anyone go back in their crease and hit yorkers over long-off and long-on. He would have scored a lot more if he was batting normally and not having to worry about protecting Mikey.'

Andy Lloyd told of the confident mood in the English dressing room during that lunch break. How quickly their high spirits would change.

'We had a very good lunch that day,' Lloyd said. 'The body language was good, we were all very confident. Nobody anticipated what was to come. I have never seen batting like it in those final 17 overs or so. The game has changed now and those kinds of innings are more commonplace with the advent of Twenty20, but in 1984 batsmen just didn't play like that.'

Holding probably had the best seat in the house when standing at the non-striker's end, although it wasn't the safest place to be.

'All I was asked to do by Viv, was to stay in and he did the rest,' recalled Holding. 'I didn't actively try to score a run until Viv thought we had reached a safe score.

'My biggest problem was trying to back up so that we could keep getting two runs each time the ball went into the deep without getting to the boundary and at the same time making sure I could get out of the way if Viv blasted the ball straight down the pitch in my direction.'

England off-spinner Geoff Miller was spared the worst of the brutality as he was bowled out early on after a tidy spell.

Miller had been recalled after 18 months on the sidelines and was only playing because of an injury to Vic Marks. The Somerset man suffered a bruised hip when struck by a Courtney Walsh short ball in the tour match at Taunton days before the one-day series commenced.

It would be easy to assume Marks felt relieved to have escaped the punishment from his county team-mate that day in Manchester, but that is not how he viewed it. Further, the absence may well have cost him his Test career for he was unable to follow on from his promising batting display in Pakistan.

We cannot be sure if Marks would have been selected for the first Test but given he was the man in possession and that Miller bowled himself into the first two Tests, it's a safe assumption.

'People ask me if I was pleased to avoid that onslaught from Viv,' Marks said, 'but the ball spun and Geoff Miller bowled well there early on and proved there was an opportunity for the spinner, so I wouldn't have minded playing at all.

'I made my ODI debut against Viv and the West Indies at Lord's in 1980. He didn't smash the shit out of me that day, so I actually wouldn't have minded bowling at Viv. I would go as far as saying I would like to have been part of that match – it was quite historic. Viv was sometimes more circumspect against bowlers that didn't offer an obvious threat or rouse him in the same way as a Botham or Willis might have.'

Marks' loss was Miller's gain as he extended his Test career to 34 matches and added two more games than he had expected to feature in.

'When I came back from the Australia tour in 1982/83 I had a feeling that would be my England career done,'

Miller acknowledged. 'I did okay there but not great and we lost the Ashes 2-1, so I never expected to play again.

'So it felt like a bonus to play against the West Indies. Fortunately, I managed to get out of the attack before Viv really got going. In fact, I took 3-32 but it should have been four but David Bairstow, God bless him, missed a stumping to Viv off me when he had 50-odd.'

It was Richards' one moment of fortune as Miller had got one to turn to outside leg stump in the days before leg-side wides were so severe. Richards missed his attempted flick through midwicket and Bairstow couldn't make the most of the opportunity.

'It was a leg-side stumping so wasn't easy,' Derek Pringle said, 'but Viv had lunged so far down the pitch that had David gathered it, it would have been a comfortable stumping. But he didn't manage it. It gripped quite a bit for the spinner that day and Dusty was turning it.'

So, what was England's plan to dismiss King Viv?

Derek Pringle: 'Beefy said, "Lads, keep bouncing him, he'll miss one in a minute." But he didn't.'

David Gower: 'People asked me over the years if I tried to exploit his weaknesses. What weaknesses? If you bowled him a straight one with a little bit of in-duck and he misses it, you've got a chance. But how often did he miss it? Not often. He whipped straight balls over square leg or drove it back over the bowler's head, depending on the length.

'We tried to limit him by bowling one side of the wicket but even that wasn't enough to keep Viv quiet. Great players find a way. A lot of head-scratching went on as to what we should do next. Pring was a very intelligent one-day bowler and Beefy was Beefy and capable of anything, but against Viv any normal plans went out of the window.'

Mike Gatting: 'It was almost pointless bowling at Viv, so we tried to bowl more at Mikey, but Viv was very good at getting a single at the end of the over to keep the strike. Viv was never going to get out and the way he farmed the strike was unbelievable. They were both very quick between the wickets so were able to get the ones and twos they were looking for.'

Derek Pringle: 'Whatever stage you bowl to him in any match he would always try to put you under pressure as a bowler. This day was no different, though maybe he tried to smash us *every* ball rather than *most* balls.

'You felt you had a chance against Viv, though, because he would back away and show you his stumps so you felt tempted to bowl at his stumps, but he would then smash you over long-off. We knew it just took one mistake and we'd be back in the game, but it never came. And when it did, we didn't take the chance!'

The final word from Mike Gatting: 'At the end of what was a quite unbelievable day it felt so disappointing because we had not been in that position for such a long time against the West Indies and I couldn't help thinking to myself at 160/9, "We're not only beating them, we're murdering them." But Viv had other ideas.'

The Trent Bridge Anomaly

'Gower was not naïve enough to think one win would translate into a summer-changing landmark'

How peculiar that in a summer of West Indies dominance, the one match England managed to win few could recall too much about.

'I don't remember much of that game,' West Indies wicketkeeper-batsman Jeffrey Dujon quipped, but with a genuine honesty.

On England's part, was it a case of punch-drunkenness, for they received such a pounding with bat and ball it is of little wonder their three-wicket victory at Nottingham barely registered in the memory banks.

This match, the second of three one-day internationals where England drew level in the series before going down at Lord's, was responsible for prefixing West Indies' 'invincible' status in 1984 with 'almost'.

'I don't remember it being too memorable,' said England seamer Neil Foster, 'but I do recall bowling a lot at Clive Lloyd and keeping him quiet on what was a low, slow wicket. They liked the ball coming on more and for once our bowlers performed well on a pitch that did a bit.'

David Gower was not naïve enough to think one win would translate into a summer-changing landmark but still, he would have been thankful for its timing. He had been installed as Bob Willis's successor as the official captain but only for the one-day series initially. The win persuaded the Test and County Cricket Board hierarchy to extend his reign until the end of the international summer, before further review.

To say it was a tough gig for Gower to start out with as skipper would be a serious understatement. 'Every day, every session, every ball, was a challenge against the West Indies at that time,' said England's off-spin all-rounder, Geoff Miller.

'Whether you were bowling against them or batting, it was always a challenge because of the quality of their players and the strength in depth that they had. Not only did they have great fast bowlers in the side, look at the quality of the fast bowlers who couldn't get in, like Courtney Walsh and Wayne Daniel.'

Gower won the toss and elected to send the tourists into bat on a pitch that threatened to seam around, which it duly did. West Indies were all out for 179 with 6.3 overs remaining. Medium-pacer Derek Pringle was the pick of the pack for England with figures of 3-21 from ten overs.

'There was a bit more in the pitch for the seam bowlers,' Pringle reflected, 'and it helped that Viv didn't get going when he swept one off Dusty (Miller) and got a top edge to me at square leg. It was nice to beat them.'

England were strolling to victory at 131/2 before a late collapse made the match slightly more tense than it might have been. The openers Graeme Fowler and Andy Lloyd combined in a solid partnership of 75 to help settle any nerves that can sometimes occur when chasing a small total.

Lloyd's 49 was not enough for him to pip Pringle to the man of the match award, but nonetheless was a crucial innings for him personally and pretty much secured his position in the Test team. He consolidated that with another top score of 37 in the deciding one-dayer at Lord's.

'It was obviously a big chunk of the runs we needed to win that match but it doesn't feature too prominently in my memory bank,' Lloyd recalled. 'I know we were always up with the rate because we weren't chasing a big total. We batted quite sensibly and did what we needed to do to win.'

It was always likely to be a season of potential opportunities for Warwickshire's Lloyd having been 12th man for the New Zealand Test at Lord's in 1983. That he was selected for the traditional county curtain-raiser in April – MCC against champion county Essex – was further evidence that he was very much on the selectors' radar.

The left-handed Lloyd scored 60 in the first innings and an unbeaten 102 in the second, under the watchful gaze of MCC skipper Gower. So the signs were good for Lloyd.

'I saw David (Gower) in the lift at the hotel before that MCC match and he just said, "Play well mate, get some runs and I'm sure you'll get your chance because you should have played by now." That was nice to hear.

'It helped that when I did get to play against the West Indies, I had already played against most of their bowlers in county cricket. The main difference here was that there were four of them, not one, and they would have been trying a lot harder, one would imagine.

'But it still gave me a better idea of my approach, so I knew what balls to look out for to hit and I knew what I was going to block or leave. My game was well organised in my head: I wasn't a hooker so there was no way I was taking them on with that shot, though if it wasn't too short and was straight or on leg stump, I would look to get inside and run it down to fine leg.

'Anything on my legs I was looking to get away whether it was in the air or not. If it was short on the off side I would look to give it a huge whack over the top. I was looking to play back most of the time but also prepared to get forward to the pitched-up ball.'

Gower acknowledged that in those days, success in one-day internationals for a fledgling England cricketer would often lead to a Test match opportunity, as became the case with Lloyd.

'If someone was playing well for his county the general feeling was to showcase them in an ODI and see how they went before the Test series,' Gower said. 'If they showed the right temperament and ability, it was likely they would end up in the Test team, which is exactly what happened to me.' (Gower scored 114 not out in his second ODI against Pakistan.)

The selectors and senior players within the team soon identified that the opening partnership between Fowler and Lloyd, two left-handers, was showing promise for the longer term. They put on 75 at Trent Bridge and then 60 at Lord's.

'They had contrasting styles but were effective,' said Pringle. 'Foxy jumped around a lot and played his shots while Andy had a lower sense of gravity, didn't jump around and looked very composed.'

Pringle was another to further his reputation in the Trent Bridge match. He was still fighting an internal battle over whether he was trying to be a hit-the-deck seamer or a medium-pace swinger. He himself felt more the latter and in time he would prove that to be true. But in the early 1980s, influences at Essex as well as Bob Willis were still urging him to run in and bowl quickly. He knew his back would never have stood up to that over time.

Pringle was never going to be 'another Ian Botham' but was probably the first in a long line subsequent to him to suffer from that uncomfortable comparison. Maybe the only likeness was that both swung the ball prodigiously in helpful conditions.

'I always found it intriguing that Botham and I could co-exist in the same team, though I wasn't as good a batsman as he was,' Pringle acknowledged, adding that Botham was a helpful team-mate without being pushy with his opinions.

'Mostly he let you get on with your own game. But if he liked you, he was generous with his time and advice, as most players were. The papers called me "the new Botham" but I don't think it bothered Ian too much, as it shouldn't have done.'

One negative from England's day in Nottingham surrounded struggling batsman Mike Gatting. He walked into bat with a chorus of boos ringing round Trent Bridge after he was selected ahead of local cult hero Derek Randall.

It didn't help Gatting's cause that he perished to Joel Garner for the second straight match for single figures (0 and 6). He was dropped for the decider at Lord's, where Randall played and scored 8.

The third one-day international, the decider, was a nondescript eight-wicket victory for the West Indies. England struggled to 196/9 off their allotted 55 overs as not one batsman reached 40. Joel Garner's analysis of 1-17 from his 11 overs summed up the hardship facing England, as these fast bowlers were not only fearsome but deadly accurate with it.

Viv Richards' 84 not out from just 65 deliveries saw him warm up for the first Test in ominously destructive form. But everyone had come to expect that type of performance from the Antiguan 'Master Blaster' by then.

Maybe the one memorable event of the third ODI was the fielding of Roger Harper. He was starting to develop a reputation as being the best fielder in the world and he fully justified the hype at the home of cricket.

Harper not only caught Botham running in from the midwicket boundary after a mistimed pull shot off Eldine Baptiste, but also spectacularly ran out Allan Lamb off the first ball after the lunch interval.

'I knew Lamby would be looking to get off the mark,' Harper recalled, 'so I bowled him a ball just short of a length on off stump and I anticipated where he would play it and took off there immediately, between cover and point.

'I got there quickly, and once I picked up and hit the stumps at the bowler's end it was clear that he was in trouble.'

Conclusively, the one-day series revealed enough to demonstrate how difficult England would find things in the five-match Test series, for they failed to register 200 on any occasion.

Dujon believes the unbelievable win in Manchester deflated the home team and added further belief to the tourists' initial expectation – that they would not only win both the ODI and Test series but win them well.

'I was confident we would win the Test series, though obviously never knew by what margin,' Dujon said. 'The confidence I had in what we were capable of was heightened after Old Trafford. That we were still able to get over the line despite being in such bad trouble boosted us even more and probably demoralised England.

'They struggled to keep to a settled team throughout the series. They had too many people playing for places, and they knew once they came into the team they had to do well, or they would get dropped. We were aware of that and took advantage as best we could.'

The Edgbaston Chronicles, First Test

'England Outplayed, Out-thought by Ruthless Windies'

*'They were desperate for balance and solidity in their
batting and bowling, but it was always going to be
difficult to find that against the quality that we had.
There was a lot of pressure on them, especially the new
players, and we tried to maintain that at all times'* –
Jeffrey Dujon

England knew they faced an ominous task against the
West Indies in this Test series yet there was a feeling in
both camps they had already resigned themselves to a
painful series defeat before it had even started.

'England gave the impression (at Edgbaston) they
had not expected anything other than a beating and they
duly got it,' Malcolm Marshall later reflected in his 1987
autobiography, *Marshall Arts*.

The West Indies won by an innings and 180 runs,
which was then England's fourth-heaviest defeat ever and
took West Indies' unbeaten sequence to 19 in Tests.

David Gower won the toss and did, according to
debutant and Edgbaston native Andy Lloyd, what most
Warwickshire captains would have done, which was to
bat first. Yet they crashed to 191 all out before the West

Indies racked up a mammoth total of 606 all out. England capitulated again in the second innings, for 245.

Derek Pringle played in the first three Tests of the series and he was realistic, albeit defeatist, in his honest reflections of the task that faced England that summer.

'We all knew that with the battery of fast bowlers they had, they would be extremely difficult to beat because there were no limitations on bouncers then,' Pringle said. 'Unless you can keep hooking them out of the ground, which is very difficult, you have to find a way to survive as they never bowled many balls in your half.

'You had to be a good puller, hooker and cutter but because they were so accurate, they didn't give you much to cut so that left the pull and hook shot. Lamby was good in that regard, so was Gower. But it was still going to be very hard work to get on top of them. They would have had to fail spectacularly with the bat and then you would have to bat extremely well and then you might be able to ram the advantage home to win. But generally both of those scenarios were unlikely, so I don't think we honestly expected to beat them in this series.'

It would be difficult to be overly critical of Gower and his team due to the simple fact they were outplayed by a superior team, possibly the greatest of all time. But perhaps areas they were found wanting surrounded preparation and self-belief. Most successful professional sportspeople would say if the odds are stacked against you, you still have to believe victory is possible. Against this West Indies team, though, reality appeared to hold sway over belief.

Gower insisted he always tried to be upbeat in team talks and pre-match dinners, but some of his team-mates detected defeatism and negativity from the start, not just from Gower but generally around the camp. Allan Lamb said there was rarely any talk of winning throughout the series, while Chris Broad, who came into the team for the second Test, remembered the general objective being more about not losing, than winning.

'I became a captain (of Warwickshire) down the line and would never have created the atmosphere that was around then,' said Andy Lloyd, who was making his debut in the match. 'It was all very negative. The message was, "We've just got to try and compete and hold our own." There was no talk of taking the game to the opposition or trying to win and I couldn't believe that.

'I have always been a glass half full person and that's the way I have lived my life. I would always work out a way of how to win, always, and if you can't win, then don't lose. Obviously, it was going to be difficult against that great team, but you must be positive.'

Lamb alluded to possible psychological scarring from the ODI defeat at Old Trafford, as that really was a morale-sapper having been so well placed for victory before Viv Richards' magical innings.

'We should have beaten them at Old Trafford,' Lamb said. 'Thereafter, everyone had a negative attitude thinking, "We're never going to beat them." I heard these comments all the time. "My God, it's the West Indies, how are we ever going to beat them?" You could feel and sense that the belief wasn't there, which made things even more difficult.'

The lack of preparation cannot be placed at Gower's door for the situation dictated, as it did every year, that England's players met up for the first time together as a team the afternoon before the Test match (or series). They had played the Texaco Trophy one-day series, with the same nucleus of players it must be said, but in terms of the longer format England met up for the first time to make plans on how to beat the mighty West Indies at 3pm the day before the series began.

The West Indies by then had played four three-day games against Worcestershire, Somerset, Glamorgan and Northamptonshire, a two-day game against Oxford and Cambridge Universities and two one-day matches, as well as the one-day series against England. They were already a well-oiled machine over many years and were now totally prepared for the Test series with England. Joel Garner said the main messages from their team meetings leading up to the first Test were that overconfidence would be their greatest threat; that the bowlers had to 'take care' of Gower, Lamb and Botham; it was up to the batsmen to 'collar' Bob Willis. They didn't do a bad job on all counts.

It was not an ideal situation for a new England captain to inherit.

'We would always arrive about 3pm on a Wednesday afternoon after playing a county match, then be ready to net about 3.30,' Derek Pringle recalled. 'There would be a team dinner on the night (at Birmingham's Plough & Harrow Hotel then) with sumptuous food, wine and port. Then, in a cursory manner, tactics would be discussed over dinner.

'There weren't any whiteboards like you see today but there was a plan. I remember Gower emphasising to the bowlers, "To Viv Richards you've got to bowl at least another set of stumps wide of off stump. He's brilliant at whipping it over square leg for four."'

Gower's recollections concurred with Pringle's in that preparations were rushed, and hardly ideal to go into a series against the West Indies.

'That's the way things were done in those days,' Gower said, 'because you might not finish a county match until the Tuesday evening. There was just enough time to meet on Wednesday for a bit of a net, take a few catches, have a cup of tea and then the team dinner on the night.'

The impression of defeatism that some players had might reflect a little harshly on Gower, yet he was embarking on his first Test as the official England captain. There was very little time to work on tactics and, crucially, he had a laid-back manner that was his way of empowering his team to be more accountable as individuals, although others interpreted this casual approach as lacking in strong leadership.

'You would have an up and at 'em, let's back ourselves-type speech at dinner,' Gower explained, 'but the way I approached my time in captaincy, when I had some good and some bad days, was to listen to the lads you're working with.

'When we're thinking of how we're going to get Greenidge and Haynes out, I'm not going to tell my bowler what to do. I'm going to work with him and give him the field he thinks gives him the best chance of doing that.

'Bowlers at Test match level are not machines that you feed data to and order them to bowl in a certain way, and my bowling record was not good. They are skilled sportsmen, so my preferred way was to work with them and manoeuvre enough between us to try to bring about the best approach for that bowler in the field.'

The consensus from the England camp is that it was agreed the night before the series that Essex seamer Neil Foster would play at Edgbaston, yet on the morning of the match, he was omitted in favour of the second spinner, Nick Cook, which many felt was the wrong call.

'I felt sorry for Fozzy,' Pringle said, 'but it was funny in a way because he was going to drive us both to Birmingham, before deciding it was a bad idea as he thought I would likely be the 12th man and would have no way of getting back, so we both drove. Then Fozzy was made 12th man and had to drive home alone!'

Foster learned not to take his place for granted and with good reason having taken a five-wicket haul in the previous Test in Lahore. Different opposition, different conditions yes, but still it wasn't an ideal way to encourage a young Test hopeful.

'The selection policy was up the creek,' Foster recalled. 'Nobody's place was safe apart from a few senior players, maybe. The reason I was in the side was because of that ongoing transition. Even a few of our senior players weren't as good as they used to be, and Ian Botham would be an example of that.

'We weren't a very good side, and we were trying to clutch at straws. You could say Gower, Botham, Lamb and Willis were guaranteed the first three Tests but for everybody else it was a free-for-all.'

One player who benefitted from that selection chaos was wicketkeeper Paul Downton, who had been overlooked for the Texaco Trophy matches when David Bairstow played. The Yorkshireman disappointed with scores of 13, 9 and 8 and a crucial missed stumping when Viv Richards scored his unbeaten 189 at Old Trafford.

Downton, therefore, was recalled for the first Test having developed his game since being dropped after the first Ashes Test in 1981. Although Downton had given an earlier positive account of himself in the West Indies in 1980/81, England possibly came too early for him then after he had swapped Kent for Middlesex to change his status from 'Alan Knott's deputy'.

'It was a major blow to have to spend three years out of the team,' Downton admitted. 'Unfortunately, I dropped Allan Border, one of seven catches that we put down, in my one Test in the 1981 Ashes at Trent Bridge and I was one of the casualties.

'I was forced to find my feet as a professional cricketer and went to Brisbane to play club cricket for a couple of winters and coached Stellenbosch University the winter after that. I started to develop my batting more at Middlesex and enjoyed my role in what was a very successful team. By 1984, my game was in a good place.'

The inconsistent selection policy that was going on around the England team was not lost on the West Indies. Like the true, ruthless champions they were, Clive Lloyd encouraged his team to be professional and make the most of every opportunity to rub England's noses in the dirt. The 150-run partnership at Edgbaston between numbers nine and ten, Eldine Baptiste and Michael Holding, in their first innings was a perfect example.

'After Bob Willis had taken two early wickets, they allowed us to build a colossal total,' Malcolm Marshall said. 'The bowling was dreadfully wayward and it seemed to us that England, defending a small total, were going through the motions, hoping for wickets rather than planning for them. They were thoroughly demoralised when they came off the field.'

Jeffrey Dujon was slightly more sympathetic but, equally, he revealed how the West Indies identified that sense of mayhem in and around the England camp and were intent on exploiting it.

'It was a time of transition for them,' observed Dujon. 'Bob Willis had been around a long time, Geoff Miller had been in and out of the team, others were in the same position. They were desperate for balance and solidity in their batting and bowling.'

England made the worst possible start, reduced to 5/2 with the wickets of Graeme Fowler and Derek Randall and that was effectively 20/3 when Andy Lloyd was struck on his right temple by a Marshall bouncer that forced him to retire hurt. Tragically, he wouldn't face another ball in Test cricket.

Allan Lamb and Gower soon followed to make it 49/4, plus Lloyd. Ian Botham's plucky innings of 64 brought minor respectability but their total was never going to be competitive. Gower knew he had been misled by the pitch, though the two bowling attacks were worlds apart in quality.

'It was a slow, low pitch, had a bit of moisture in it and seamed a bit,' Gower said. 'It was one of those scenarios where you hope to just have a bit of luck in the morning session and get through. It certainly wasn't a pitch where it was going to be taking your head off from a good length. By the time they batted, the pitch was mighty flat.'

Lamb's struggles continued, following on from a fruitless winter. Curiously, by the end of his career he never managed a single half-century at Edgbaston in his five Tests on the ground, where he averaged just 13 in total. 'I don't know why but I never seemed to get runs there, because it was always a flat wicket,' Lamb said, 'but it wasn't a happy hunting ground for me. It was a strange one.'

Larry Gomes (143) and Viv Richards (117) had no such issues, as they piled on the agony for Gower and England, laying a foundation for the West Indies that meant it would always be difficult for the home team to fight back.

'Viv whipped me over square leg,' recalled Pringle, 'and Gower ran up and said, "Remember what we spoke about?" I told him to go and ask Paul Downton what the line was, as it was way outside off stump.' It summed up the margin of error permissible for England's bowlers.

The lower order runs from Baptiste, with a Test best of 87 not out, and Holding, with an aggressive 69 that included four of the five sixes in the innings, were less like a dagger through England's heart and more like death from a thousand cuts. It was pure humiliation and the kind of ruthlessness that Lloyd had demanded from his side.

'Lloydy spoke to me, Mikey, Roger, Malcolm and Joel in practice and told us that our job was not only to take five wickets, but we should also be trying to score a fifty,' Baptiste revealed. 'We all took that attitude into the match.

'Mikey walked in and said, "Soca," which was my nickname, "do you want to score a hundred?" I said, "Yeah, of course." So, he said, "Right then, let's both get a hundred." I was a little apprehensive at first and was batting to not get out and Mikey spotted that and urged me to be more aggressive. We then started to get on top of them.'

Lloyd maintains the runs from Baptiste and Holding were not by coincidence and their batting efforts were the result of lots of time in the nets.

'Those lower order runs happened a lot, our bowlers loved to bat,' Lloyd said. 'In fact, when we practised in the nets one thing I used to like to do was to put our bowlers into bat first and have them face new balls to practise against. They needed to get used to playing against good bowling with new balls so there could be no excuses when the games came around that they were not prepared for it.'

Pringle finished with a five-wicket haul in the innings, but it wasn't a career milestone that he felt he could, or should, celebrate too much given the circumstances.

'It felt a little bit empty but it's always nice to get a five-for,' he said. 'I remember Ray Illingworth writing in a newspaper column that I should be dropped. I thought,

"Blimey, I've taken a five-for and he still wants me dropped!'"

Pringle was not rushing in and trying to bowl as quickly as he had the previous summer, on Willis's advice, but he was still trying to bowl a quicker pace than he felt comfortable at, around 82–83mph, which he knew was never going to worry the likes of Richards.

'The penny gradually dropped some time after this series that fast bowling was for idiots and if I carried on like this I probably had another three years left,' Pringle revealed. 'I knew I was going to be more of a swing bowler, but I didn't learn to really swing the ball until I spoke to Phil Newport in 1989 when he showed me how to grip the ball.'

The first Test match was not just about West Indian dominance and England's meek surrender. There were a few tense moments along the way. The tourists' pace spearhead Malcolm Marshall was twice warned by umpire Dickie Bird for overdoing the short-pitched tactics, especially at Ian Botham. Marshall felt it was a genuine ploy to dismiss Botham, as he struggled to resist the hook shot. Fortunately for the bowler, Botham was less irritated by the bouncers and the issue gradually fizzled out.

Downton's fighting spirit with the bat in both innings (33 and 56) was one of the few plus points for England. With Alan Knott banned for touring South Africa with the rebels, and with Bob Taylor seemingly also nearing retirement, Downton sensed an opportunity and did himself a lot of good in a losing case.

'I had a really good net before the match at Edgbaston and felt in form,' Downton recalled. 'It helped that I had played three Tests in the West Indies in our previous series against them, so it gave me an idea of what to expect. On that occasion I batted all afternoon to see out a draw with David Gower. I only made 26 not out but I spent three hours at the crease and took some confidence from that. I felt confident that I had a reasonable defence against pace.

'It was a no-lose situation having been promoted from number nine. I enjoyed the opportunity to open and played nicely, never gave a chance, put the bad ball away with an attacking field allowing good value for your shots. I was enjoying being back in Test cricket. What annoyed me, though, was getting out to Harper (caught) having fought so hard against the fast bowlers.'

Marshall was at the forefront of West Indian mischief with the ball all summer but in this match, it was the 6ft 9in Somerset paceman Joel Garner who troubled England the most with his pace and unerring accuracy that gave them absolutely nothing. He accounted for nine English wickets.

'Although it had been a bit like participating in a commando raid on an undefended village, I was totally satisfied with the outcome,' Garner said in his autobiography *Big Bird Flying High* years later.

Garner was well accustomed to bowling in English conditions. After all, he helped beat the Australian tourists in 1977 on his Somerset debut with six wickets; in his next match he took eight wickets on his County Championship debut against Warwickshire; and in the following game took a career-best 8-31 in only his second Championship match, against Glamorgan.

Garner was handed the new ball in this series, which was still quite a new initiative as the West Indies went. Previously it had usually been two of Marshall, Holding and Roberts. Playing for the West Indies was a real badge of honour for Garner and those who knew him best feel that when Lloyd trusted him with the new ball he raised his game – and his speeds.

'He was hostile, he would hit the splice of the bat, he always knew where it was going, he would have been a nightmare to face and fortunately I didn't have to face him much being his team-mate for many years,' said Somerset and England all-rounder Vic Marks.

'Holding would glide in, Marshall was almost poetic, their actions were classical and maybe the batsmen were able to line them up even if facing them wasn't any easier. Joel was slightly less aesthetically pleasing in terms of his action but no less effective. In terms of difficulty, Joel would be right up there.

'He was a lovely guy, and sometimes we thought he was a bit too soft on batsmen and lacking the ruthlessness of a Colin Croft maybe. But I am sure he was more aggressive when he bowled for the West Indies, due to that natural competitiveness amongst their attack.'

The media reaction after this match was as hard-hitting in its criticism of England's performance as it was complimentary in its acknowledgement that this West Indies team was as good as any team, anywhere.

Clive Lloyd, like a prudent football manager well-schooled in psychology, refused to allow his players to soak up the hype too much. He kept insisting the margin of defeat did not truly reflect the difference between the teams and that his own side needed to keep finding improvement from somewhere.

From where, exactly, would have been a fair question.

EDGBASTON SCORECARD:

England

	First Innings			Second Innings	
G. Fowler	c Dujon b Garner	0	lbw b Garner		7
T.A. Lloyd	retired hurt	10	absent hurt		
D.W. Randall	b Garner	0	c Lloyd b Garner		1
D.I. Gower	c Harper b Holding	10	c Dujon b Garner		12
A.J. Lamb	c Lloyd b Baptiste	15	c Richards b Marshall		13
I.T. Botham	c Garner b Harper	64	lbw b Garner		38
G. Miller	c Dujon b Garner	22	c Harper b Marshall		11
D.R. Pringle	c Dujon b Holding	4	not out		46
P.R. Downton	lbw b Garner	33	(2) c Greenidge b Harper		56
N.G.B. Cook	c Lloyd b Marshall	2	(9) run out		9
R.G.D. Willis	not out	10	(10) c Dujon b Garner		22
59.3 overs, 21 extras		191	76.5 overs, 20 extras		235

Fall of wickets, 1st Innings: 1-1 (Fowler); 2-5 (Randall); 2-20* (Lloyd ret. hurt); 3-45 (Lamb); 4-49 (Gower); 5-89 (Miller); 6-103 (Pringle); 7-168 (Botham); 8-173 (Cook); 9-191 (Downton)

Bowling: Marshall 14-4-37-1; Garner 14.3-2-53-4; Holding 16-4-44-2; Baptiste 11-3-28-1; Harper 4-1-8-1

Fall of wickets, 2nd Innings: 1-17 (Fowler); 2-21 (Randall); 3-37 (Gower); 4-65 (Lamb); 5-127 (Botham); 6-138 (Miller); 7-181 (Downton); 8-193 (Cook); 9-235 (Willis)

Bowling: Marshall 23-7-65-2; Garner 23.5-7-55-5; Holding 12-3-29-0; Baptiste 5-1-18-0; Harper 13-3-48-1

West Indies

	First Innings:	
C.G. Greenidge	lbw b Willis	19
D.L. Haynes	lbw b Willis	8
H.A. Gomes	c Miller b Pringle	143
I.V.A Richards	c Randall b Cook	117
P.J. Dujon	c Gower b Miller	23

C.H. Lloyd	c Pringle b Botham	71
M.D. Marshall	lbw b Pringle	2
R.A. Harper	b Pringle	14
E.A.E. Baptiste	not out	87
M.A. Holding	c Willis b Pringle	69
J. Garner	c Lamb b Pringle	0
143 overs, 53 extras,		606

Fall of wickets: 1-34 (Haynes); 2-35 (Greenidge); 3-241 (Richards); 4-294 (Dujon); 5-418 (Gomes); 6-418 (Lloyd); 7-421 (Marshall); 8-455 (Harper); 9-605 (Holding); 10-606 (Garner)

Bowling: Willis 25-3-108-2; Botham 34-7-127-1; Pringle 31-5-108-5; Cook 38-6-127-1; Miller 15-1-83-1

Toss: England, elected to bat first

Player of the match: Larry Gomes

West Indies won by an innings and 180 runs

The Graveyard Series for Outgoing England Stars

'I'm not going to sit here apologising for every selectorial decision or error that may or may not have cost players their career. You make these decisions at the time for the right reasons, whether they work or not.' – David Gower

It was not unusual for the West Indies to expose vulnerabilities in opposition teams during their pomp in the 1980s. But it was unprecedented for so many international careers to be threatened or ended in one match or series, as happened in 1984.

Derek Randall's struggle at Edgbaston did for his England career; Andy Lloyd's sickening injury in the same game meant he was unable to play Test cricket again; all-rounder Geoff Miller was discarded for good after playing in the first two matches; Bob Willis retired after the third Test when he was averaging 61 in the series with the ball; Paul Terry never returned after breaking his arm in the fourth Test, his second; and even Chris Tavare's career was almost done after he played in the fifth Test, with a subsequent five-year hiatus separating this summer and his final Test in 1989.

Even Mike Gatting's England career appeared to be in jeopardy after he twice shouldered arms at Lord's only to be dismissed lbw twice for low scores. He was fortunate that David Gower fought for his recall and inclusion in the India tour squad, where he was a success and able to rebuild his international career from there.

West Indies, strangely, had a victim of their own from the series as Eldine Baptiste played a part in all five wins yet was dropped thereafter and did not feature again for six years. And even then, it was only for one more match. But this graveyard of a series was mainly about the demise of England players.

Derek Randall

Randall, known as 'Arkle' or 'Rags', was one of the most popular cricketers of his generation such was his occasional magic with the bat, all-round quirkiness and exuberance in the field. He was simply 'a character' and maybe one of the last of his kind before the game was transformed into a more ultra-professional version.

Randall was something of an enigma, unfortunately possessing more Test ducks than any other specialist batter over the course of his career (14) yet was good enough to make incredible scores such as the 174 against Australia in Melbourne. There, at the MCG, he came in at number three with the score 28/1 and it was 346/5 when he departed. Undaunted by the target of 463, England fell just 45 runs short.

In that innings, he had to cope with a barrage of hostile short balls from Dennis Lillee on his way to what was his highest Test score and one delivery struck him on the head. In keeping with his usual humour, Randall is believed to have said, 'There is no point hitting me there, there's nothing in it.' He also scored 150 against the Australians at Sydney when batting for almost ten hours, again at number three. Curiously, his 47th and final Test match was his first against the West Indies.

It was an uncomfortable, forgettable match for him personally and the team. He lasted three deliveries in the first innings before he was bowled by Joel Garner for a duck. Then he took nine balls in the second innings for one run when he edged to Clive Lloyd at first slip, again off Garner.

'I'm not going to sit here apologising for every selectorial decision or error that may or may not have cost players their career,' said David Gower, when asked about Randall being dropped after the first Test at Edgbaston. 'You make these decisions at the time for the right reasons, whether they work or not.'

There was some debate as to whether Randall was the right candidate to bat at three but, as detailed above, his two best innings in Australia were made at three against some mighty fast bowlers. The manner of his dismissal in the second innings, backing away, before being caught at first slip, didn't look good.

Gower added: 'He was fidgety against quick bowling and between me and the selectors we were trying to work out where was the best place for me to bat. We thought if I batted three it might be a bit rushed to run off the field and then pad up and potentially be straight out there if we lost an early wicket, so we tried to persuade someone else to bat three.

'Derek would probably have been happier at four or five, but we stuck him in at three. If he minded, he didn't show it publicly. It happened to me before in Australia and didn't work yet I eventually came back and had the best years of my career in that position. If you can get your head around it quickly, it's not too bad. But when you're playing the West Indies, the words head and quickly have a different meaning.'

This West Indies team was said to be able to 'smell fear' better than any other and if they ever detected that anyone was uncertain about facing up to their pace attack, they heightened their aggression to show complete ruthlessness. Randall apparently gave off those vibes, according to Malcolm Marshall, whether or not it was an accurate impression.

'I can always sense when a batsman is apprehensive,' Marshall said a couple of years after the series, 'and among those I'm convinced has no stomach for the fast stuff is Derek Randall. Yet he is such a clown I cannot be sure if he was trying to con me. For a man who might not relish the truly fast bowling, though, he certainly piled up some runs over the years.'

Jeffrey Dujon admitted there was 'a whole lot of pressure on Randall to perform and it must have taken its toll', but acknowledged he had faced sustained fast bowling previously and was successful in Australia. Dujon was alluding to the selection merry-go-round that was English cricket then. They were aware of the chop-and-change mentality and looked to exploit it.

'It would have been difficult for him to succeed against the pressure we applied and with the selection the way it was with England,' Dujon commented. 'It wasn't a situation I would have fancied.'

Randall's county team-mate Tim Robinson insisted that while Randall was once a very competent player of pace bowling, the situation changed once he was struck in the mouth by a Michael Holding bouncer when an England XI was playing against Tasmania on the 1982/83 tour of Australia. Randall had since admitted the blow knocked him back over his stumps and put him in hospital for a week.

'I think Rags lost a bit of confidence against the quicker bowlers once Holding hit him on a bad wicket in Australia,' Robinson said. 'After that he'd gone and didn't want to know (pace). I remember when Notts would play Derbyshire, Rags would be hanging out the window waiting to see if they were playing Wrighty (John Wright) or if Mikey was playing. If it was Mikey, Rags started to feel a dodgy hamstring coming on!

'This Edgbaston Test match was enough for him. But in fairness, he was still capable of scoring runs at Notts.

Some days he could be a genius and on other days he wasn't at his best.

'He was a one-off.'

The summer of '84 might not have been Randall's finest hour, but it's important his legacy is not completely tarnished for he was once a warrior of a batsman for England in the middle order as those 150s showed.

'I remember batting with him in Perth against Lillee and (Geoff) Lawson and they were bouncing and sledging the shit out of him, and he just loved it,' recalled Derek Pringle. 'He played brilliantly. So, it's a weird thing that he seemed more cowed by the West Indies guys than he did the Aussies on their own turf. I don't know why.'

Andy Lloyd

While it is a well-known fact that Lloyd retired hurt 10 not out on Test debut at his home ground in the first Test against the West Indies when he misjudged a short ball from Malcolm Marshall and was struck on the right temple. That was the end of his Test career.

What is less well known, in fact even the player could not recall during his interview for this book, is that Lloyd also retired hurt on the same ground against the same opposition and the same bowler four years earlier on the West Indians' 1980 tour.

Lloyd, when on 24, was hit behind the pad on his knee and suffered serious bruising. Coincidentally, his team-mate John Claughton also hurt his knee in that game but much more seriously, as he had to retire after aggravating what was a pre-existing condition.

Warwickshire opener Lloyd, with decades to have reflected on his misfortune, now makes light of his sad farewell from Test cricket.

'If I had lost my middle stump in both innings for not very much that would probably have been it anyway,' Lloyd said, 'but at least I'm a question in *Trivial Pursuit*: which England batsman was never dismissed but never got selected again?

'That wouldn't have happened unless I retired hurt on 10 not out in my only Test match. I'm a quiz answer forever.'

Team-mate Pringle remembered speaking to Lloyd after his innings of 49 at Trent Bridge in the Texaco Trophy series. Lloyd wore a helmet, but he did not wear a visor, just the earpieces. And Pringle quizzed him on why that was the case.

'I noticed that he used to sway out of the way of the ball, and I asked him why he did that,' Pringle said. 'He reasoned that was how he liked to play the short ball and I said but what happens if the ball doesn't bounce as much or swings or seams more, like it can in England. He said, "That's never happened." But in that Test match it followed him – and he had nowhere to go.'

Lloyd was playing well until the fateful delivery. He saw Graeme Fowler depart (1/1), then Randall (5/2), and at 20/2 and having batted for half an hour Lloyd expected a ball from Marshall to bounce more and not move as much as it did.

'It just angled back into me off the pitch,' Lloyd recalled. 'I was expecting it to go over my shoulder. The speed and the bounce would normally not have been a problem, but that bit of movement did me.

'When the physio Bernard Thomas came on, he was checking my vision and he asked me to read an advertising board that was for the television company in the day, Rediffusion. I couldn't read it and I then knew I was in trouble and there was something seriously wrong. I never lost consciousness, but I was always going to retire hurt because my vision was so badly affected.'

The incident happened at 11.30am and by midday Lloyd was in the Queen Elizabeth Hospital in Birmingham under the care of Professor James Crews, who was an expert in these types of injuries.

'He explained to me that the impact of the blow on my head had basically destroyed about 35 per cent of the mechanisms behind my right eye that send messages to the brain. The vision was worse initially and he told me that I wouldn't get all that vision back. He was exactly right.'

Lloyd spent a week in hospital and, when Pringle paid him a visit, he remembered Lloyd's face being heavily swollen and in something of a mess.

'His face was huge with the swelling, one eye was closed, and the other was all bloodshot,' Pringle said. 'It was sad that he wasn't considered for England again. Doubly sad because up to that point he had looked composed and organised against their quick bowlers.'

The consensus was the injury was partly because of Lloyd's misjudgement and partly down to the Warwickshire pitch playing slower and lower than normal. Lloyd, after all, was well accustomed to opening the batting at

Edgbaston. Allan Lamb also suggested that Marshall 'was a skidder' and his bouncers could arrive a little flatter and faster than many fast bowlers.

'The irony was that it was a short delivery and on most pitches what Andy did would have been fine,' according to Gower. 'But it didn't get up and he was in the wrong place at the wrong time. Andy was a good player. It was such a shame that one non-bouncing bouncer and the freakishness of the injury ended his career so abruptly. If he could have got in, scored a few fifties like Broad or Fowler, he could easily have played a few more Test matches.'

Marshall felt upset about what happened to Lloyd but attributed the blame towards the English hierarchy for preparing a slow pitch that was designed to nullify the West Indies pace bowling but only resulted in making reading the short ball much more difficult.

'Lloyd was as much a victim of the English policy on pitches as he was of a bouncer that simply never got up,' Marshall commented. 'They tried to take the sting out of our bowling by deadening the tracks but instead all that was achieved was a succession of variable and unpredictable wickets on which a batsman could never be sure of the bounce.

'Lloyd was the first casualty, and nobody was more upset about it than me and, as they helped him away for treatment, I was close to breaking down.'

Lloyd made his comeback with England A on tour to Zimbabwe in February the following year. Although he played well enough to continue his county career, he knew deep down inside that he was never going to be good enough again to return to the highest level.

'I knew I was in trouble in Zimbabwe when I tried to catch the ball in the field, and I was just hopeless – I really struggled with depth perception,' Lloyd explained. 'I didn't have it because one eye wasn't working in unison with the other, and that pretty much stayed the same for the rest of my career. Although it never stopped fast bowlers trying to bounce me and test me out, but that was their job! I worked out a way to play county cricket but was never going to be consistent enough to play Test cricket again.

'When you play at that level, you really must be at the top of your game,' he added. 'As far as coming back to Test cricket went, it wasn't going to happen, because if you had any physical defects or doubts about yourself those top teams find them out.'

Geoff Miller

The end of Miller's England career was less dramatic than Randall's and Lloyd's. There was no serious injury or dramatic sequences of play where he was subjected to a barrage of bouncers. Quite simply, he was found wanting as a Test cricketer in what were his 33rd and 34th matches.

He was certainly not too old at 31 and, against any other nation, Miller might well have proven himself a worthy England player for a while longer. But against this side he struggled to do enough to stay in the side, especially as selectors would get itchy fingers if players went two matches without making any sort of impression.

Miller, in fairness, did not expect to receive a call-up initially for the one-day series after an 18-month break from the team, but an injury to Vic Marks presented an opportunity for him.

'I soon found what quality I had, had dipped,' Miller admitted. 'I played the second Test as well at Lord's and then that was me done. I wasn't as good a player then as I had been years before. My passion to play and do well was still there but my ability had waned.'

Miller toiled for combined figures of 1-142 in the Edgbaston and Lord's Tests. It was interesting that although the experienced off-spin all-rounder was senior to fellow slow bowler Nick Cook, he never seemed to have the full backing of Gower if his tactics at Edgbaston were anything to go by.

This, in a match where England omitted seamer Neil Foster to accommodate the second spinner. When Gomes and Richards added 206 for the third wicket, Miller was not asked to bowl. Not even with the thought of the turning off-spin against the left-handed Gomes. It was not until the score was 260/3 that 'Dusty' was introduced.

Miller had another quiet match at Lord's where he scored 0 and 9 and bowled infrequently, partly because the conditions favoured the swing and seam bowlers more in the West Indies first innings and then Miller, like all his team-mates, could not contain Gordon Greenidge in the second innings and, as he said himself, 'That was me done.'

Bob Willis

Willis was 35 by the time of this series, well past his peak, and still troubled by a virus that caused him to fly home early from the Pakistan tour in April. His knees had been troublesome for much of his career, but he had learned to live with the hardship for there was no greater trier or 'hundred percenter' than Willis.

One of many examples of Willis's commitment and endeavour came a year earlier at Headingley when New Zealand claimed their first Test win on English soil. Willis took four wickets in the first innings and although the Kiwis required just 101 to win second time around, Willis gave it everything to avert defeat, bowling unchanged for his 5-35 in 14 overs. That was Bob.

Fast forward to June 1984, and it was convenient for both Gower and the selectors to retain Willis in the team rather than encourage him to slip away into the wilderness. He provided support and guidance to the new captain and though his performances had started to show signs of decline, his reputation as England's highest Test wicket-taker demanded an element of faith.

He was still threatening in bursts, and while his lionhearted approach would never fail him or his team, he no longer possessed the stamina or cutting edge to bowl quickly and accurately for sustained periods, hence his lofty bowling average of 61 in the three matches he played, the first three Tests that decided the outcome of the series and, ultimately, proved to be his farewell.

Gower had a voice in selection then and was no shrinking violet as far as his opinions on team-mates were concerned but, equally, he also knew that as a new skipper he had to be a little diplomatic with his views. He supported Willis staying on.

'You're always wary of throwing someone out too early,' Gower said. 'It is one of the hardest things as a captain and a selector to know that moment when someone has gone beyond their sell-by date. Bob was still trying very hard on pitches that weren't very Bob-friendly. He needed more pace in the pitches to be effective and we didn't want the extra pace as we had to bat against the West Indies attack. Not that I ever spoke to a groundsman about what to prepare. We still relied on Bob to give us a bit of zip. I tried to be an ally to him as he was the previous captain, but you could tell gradually that his days as a Test bowler were slipping by.

'Bob was coming to the end, but there weren't many better than Bob when he was on form – he was awesome. But against this team, if you were not totally on your game or playing at the best of your ability you were found out quite ruthlessly.'

Pringle understood why Willis was given the series to try to extend his Test career as he felt the cupboard was bare when it came to better options to take the new ball.

'Who else was there around then? Graham Dilley, yes, but he was out with a long-term injury. Maybe (David) "Teddy" Thomas, who Clive Lloyd said was the quickest white bowler he faced in county cricket. Greg Thomas was a 90 miles per hour bowler but fell down in terms of accuracy. It wasn't easy to replace a guy like Bob.'

Chris Broad was new to the England team but had been around county cricket long enough to know there were not too many better options ready to depose Willis. The seam bowling selections changed with a surprising volatility following the bans to Mike Hendrick and Chris Old. So, after Botham and Willis, many were jostling for a Test position, but few were able to nail down a regular spot.

Lamb shared Gower and Broad's view that Willis deserved the opportunity to try to roll back the years against the West Indies, in the absence of many obvious better candidates.

'Bob was knackered by then and if there were any better bowlers around, they would have played,' Lamb said. 'It summed up the lack of bowling options we had. Bob was a great bowler, had done so well for England over the years and for him to keep himself as fit as he did for so long was amazing. It was sad for him to bail out in the middle of a series like that, because he was a great friend and you care for your mates, but it was the right time.'

The Battle of the Spin Doctors

'Edmonds was the one who might justifiably have felt aggrieved at being overlooked that summer.' – Derek Pringle

It was not *quite* like a scene out of *The Deer Hunter* where American prisoners of war in Vietnam were playing Russian roulette and pointing a partially loaded pistol against their heads before pulling the trigger. But someone somewhere did have the unenviable task of bowling spin against the West Indies in 1984 – perhaps the greatest team of all time, on pitches that were none too friendly for spin bowling in the main.

Somerset off-spinner Vic Marks scored 83, 74 and 55 against Pakistan in his last three innings in Test cricket – England's three most recent Tests prior to the home summer of 1984. Statistics alone might suggest he was a tad unlucky then not to start the series against the West Indies three months later. He was selected for the one-day series initially, but a bruised hip ruled him out and allowed Geoff Miller to leapfrog him in the pecking order. Marks never did play Test cricket again, though he returned to the ODI team.

The brutal fact is, though, while Marks had batted well on batsman-friendly pitches in the subcontinent, he had not really advanced his cause with the ball.

'I scored runs in Pakistan but that wasn't my primary role,' Marks acknowledged. 'I'm well aware it would have been a very different challenge against the West Indies. It was a different team, a new English season and totally different conditions so I took nothing for granted.

'Test cricket plays so much in the mind, and I was the type to think, "Should I be playing here? Am I good enough to be here?" I guess I cleared that hurdle somewhat in Pakistan, albeit with the bat rather than the ball, so in that sense it was disappointing not to play any more Test cricket. However, if I looked at it more philosophically, I might say that had Derek Underwood and John Emburey never gone to South Africa I would never have played Test cricket at all.'

Marks claimed four wickets in those three Tests in Pakistan at an average of 65, while his spin twin Nick Cook, the left-armer from Leicestershire, couldn't stop taking wickets. He managed 14 in that series in Pakistan after taking 16 in his first two Test matches against New Zealand at the back end of the previous summer. Cook, then, was pretty much nailed on for Edgbaston, even if he was not certain to keep his place at a time of selectorial twitchiness.

The two significant questions facing the England selectors were: would they opt for two spinners at Edgbaston, or indeed throughout the series against Clive Lloyd's team of batting aggressors? And if they did decide to play a second spinner, who would accompany Cook? Marks had enjoyed a relatively successful World Cup on home soil 12 months earlier with 11 wickets, including 5-39 against Sri Lanka. This, of course, was an era when encouraging performances in limited-overs cricket could result in promotion to the Test team. But in the event, England captain David Gower and his fellow selectors chose to overlook him.

Emburey would almost certainly have received the call-up had it not been for his three-year ban for touring South Africa with the 'rebels'. Instead, they turned to another off-spinner in the shape of Derbyshire all-rounder Geoff Miller, who had not played for England for 18 months since he featured in all five of the Ashes Tests in 1982/83. His return there was moderate with bat and ball, though a 60 and a couple of 30s against the likes of Geoff Lawson, Jeff Thomson and Rodney Hogg indicated he could handle a bat when there was pace around. Miller's first-class batting average at the end of his career was 26.49 against Marks's 30.29. But stats, good or indifferent, predominantly achieved on the treadmill of county cricket did not always lead to England call-ups.

'You end up with what is available,' Gower explained. 'If you know Emburey is unavailable and you need an off-spinner, you start looking around. And Miller was an experienced player. Dusty theoretically was more of an all-rounder than Vic. Yes, Vic had been in Pakistan and got some runs there, but even Vic wouldn't have said he was the answer to all our prayers when we're playing against the West Indies.

'I know Vic scored a lot of runs in county cricket but whether it's 1984, 1994 or 2024, county cricket is not the definitive way to judge whether players will make successful Test cricketers. Vic is a lovely guy, and I had a lot of time for him as a guy and as a player he may well have done a decent job but, ultimately, they were never going to be big-spinning pitches and our need for extra runs was always going to be more important, which is where Dusty had the edge.'

So, they were the key answers to England's spin dilemma: Cook and Miller would form the spin attack behind the pace and seam of Willis, Botham and Pringle. In more recent times it has been a challenge for England captains to shoehorn at least one spinner into the side, but in 1984 there was more of a willingness to have two. With Botham batting at six, it allowed England to select five front-line bowlers and go in with a balanced team.

Subsequent Ashes series in 1985 and 1986/87 demonstrated how two quality spinners bowling in tandem could add a different, potent dimension when Emburey and Phil Edmonds came together. But in this case, they were not playing an Australia team in transition but a West Indies intent on smashing any slow bowler out of the attack.

Edmonds, meanwhile, found himself out of favour, somehow. The puzzling aspect to that was 1984 was one of Edmonds' best seasons of his career – he claimed more wickets for Middlesex in the County Championship than any other and achieved his career best of 8-53. However, he had a reputation for being anti-authoritarian which may not have served him well in the corridors of power and among the selectors. That did not include Gower, though, who argued firmly in his favour when it came to choosing the tour party to India later in the year.

'I was always fine with Philippe and was happy to take him to India the following winter,' Gower revealed. 'Him going on that tour was entirely my responsibility. The selectors would say things like, "Are you sure about him?" Because he had his arguments with (Mike) Brearley, more out of a personality clash, so Brears took against him and found it easier to keep him on the sidelines.

'I didn't have a personality clash with Philippe. He always wanted to be involved, always wanted to bowl, if things went slightly wrong, he could get a bit hot-headed maybe and show a bit of a temper. But whenever that happened when I was his captain, I would say, "Thanks Phil, have a break, see you in a mo." In India, I found him an absolute delight. That's when captaincy becomes a juggling act in terms of man-management because if you accommodate one (so-called 'difficult' player), others also think they can get away with things.'

Vic Marks and Paul Downton both identified personality clashes that did not aid Edmonds' international prospects. The Rhodesia-born bowler was seen by a select few in authority as an awkward personality, even a destructive character.

'Willis didn't seem to like him,' Marks said. 'Bob was big on the team ethos, and I think he saw Edmonds as a bit of an outsider who could be difficult to manage. Subsequently he didn't go on the 1982/83 tour, preposterously, and I went instead as a third off-spinner along with Miller and (Eddie) Hemmings. From a cricketing perspective that made no sense as Edmonds was a gifted bowler. Gower didn't feel threatened by Edmonds and, quite rightly, brought him back for India in 1984/85. Edmonds must have felt indebted to Gower for bringing him back and had a good couple of years in the England team thereafter.'

Downton was able to witness a different personality clash at Middlesex, with Brearley, who was regarded as one of England's best captains because of his ability to deal with players.

'Philippe and Brearley famously didn't get on and they were two Cambridge intellectuals who seemed to rub each other up the wrong way,' Downton revealed. 'They were very different people. I think Philippe frustrated Brearley because there were shades of the old amateur about him. All he wanted to do was bowl the perfect ball, to drift in, spin out and hit off. For someone who was so intelligent, he probably didn't have the cricket intelligence that a John Emburey possessed. They were chalk and cheese and I think that frustrated Brearley as he recognised that Edmonds was a phenomenally talented spin bowler, as he proved in subsequent series. But for that '84 summer he was still out of the picture.'

Mike Gatting, who was Edmonds' long-time county skipper, believed he was essentially a victim of often being the second choice for England when only one slow bowler was employed.

'He could be difficult, though he did play when the guys went to South Africa (in 1982),' Gatting commented. 'Quite simply, people have their favourites and when you're only playing one spinner most of the time there are not that many opportunities.'

Derek Pringle was a great admirer of Nick 'Beasty' Cook's talent, though concurred with the view that Edmonds was the one who might justifiably have felt aggrieved at being overlooked that summer.

Who else was around, and worthy of taming these ravenous, run-hungry West Indies batsmen? Eddie Hemmings was another off-spinner who played a sprinkling of Test cricket through the 1980s, though he had a five-year hiatus from the time he scored 95 as a nightwatchman against Australia in Sydney in 1982/83, to his recall match against Pakistan in Faisalabad. He never played in Gower's initial captaincy reign.

'Every time I went to Trent Bridge I found Eddie a bit of a handful actually,' Gower revealed. 'He always bowled very well against me, as he bowled well against left-handers in general. Eddie was one of those players on the county circuit who you knew was a bloody good bowler – but you didn't necessarily tag him as an international bowler.'

There was one name who came out of left field during this West Indies series. Surrey's veteran off-spinner Pat Pocock had not played Test cricket for eight years, in fact since the West Indies tour in 1976, when players such as Brian Close and John Edrich were still playing.

Pocock was approaching his 38th birthday – and was just a year younger than Derek Underwood – and had made his Test debut way back in 1968. Although there were sniggers from certain quarters of the media when Pocock was recalled, in much the same way as when Colin Cowdrey was flown out to Australia in 1974/75 when everyone thought they had seen the last of him in an England team, the humour was aimed more towards the selectors than the player. The move smacked of desperation but quite simply they just wanted someone to try to stem the tide in a series where the West Indies batsmen seemed unstoppable.

'For a long time, they were looking to pick players who batted as well like Geoff Miller, John Emburey, Vic Marks and Phil Edmonds,' Pocock said. 'I wasn't an all-rounder, but they knew what I was about and seemed to appreciate what I could give them.

'It all depended on what they wanted from a spinner. I like to think I had good control so I imagine they would have seen me as someone who might be able to limit the West Indian run rate somewhat.

'I was used to coming in and out of the side because as far back as 1968 I had taken 6-79 from 33 overs against Australia (at Old Trafford) yet was dropped for the next Test match. Colin Cowdrey wrote me a letter saying I shouldn't read too much into my non-selection and that my time would come again. Of course it wasn't easy competing with Derek Underwood for a single spin bowling position in that era.'

Pocock played in the innings defeat at Old Trafford in the fourth Test where he toiled hard for 4-121 in 45.3 overs and was good enough to dismiss Gordon Greenidge, caught behind, though it was slightly unfortunate for England that the Bajan opener had racked up 223 first. 'Percy' retained his place, though bowled just eight overs at The Oval.

He did enough to stay on for the one-off Test match against Sri Lanka at Lord's and then earn a place on the tour to India, where he bowled in tandem with Edmonds in what was a triumphant series for England. Marks was the reserve spinner also on the tour. Gower was a great admirer of the skills that Pocock brought to the team.

'Percy is one of the great enthusiasts and apart from Graeme Swann probably knows more about off-spin bowling than any who have come along since,' Gower insisted. 'He had an old-fashioned attitude and was someone you could rely on, which is why we took him to India later that year. I was still a relatively inexperienced captain, and it was good to have someone like Perce around who had barrel-loads of experience and good advice.

'He wasn't a "for fuck's sake, why aren't we doing this?" type of team-mate, he was more of a helpful constructive advisor who might say, "Skip, how about if we do it this way?" You can allow yourself to tap into that experience as a captain. I never minded those players, by the way, who did have a moan because it takes all sorts of characters to make a team and you have to manage them. But Percy was especially useful to me at that time with his experience.'

As detailed in the 'Missing Rebels, Surplus Talent' chapter, Kent's veteran left-arm spinner Derek Underwood may also have been in the mix for selection in 1984 had he not toured South Africa in 1981/82 and received a three-year ban.

'He could easily have gone to India in '84, he would certainly have been a candidate for Australia in '82/83 so by the same token I don't see why Deadly wouldn't have featured in the 1984 summer, given the way he was still bowling for Kent,' Vic Marks commented. 'The fact they turned to Percy in that series showed that age wasn't a problem for the selectors.'

So, for now, it was Cook and Miller. In the event, neither were able to repel a West Indian batting line-up that racked up over 600. Cook's 1-127 and Miller's 1-83 demonstrated the challenge that spinners faced in English seamer-friendly conditions, though Edgbaston was seen as not having much pace at the time. Cook was dropped for the next match as was the norm after a heavy defeat, though Miller won a vote of confidence to 'have another go'. He went wicketless at Lord's and didn't play another Test match.

The Lord's Chronicles, Second Test

Greenidge Finds His Zenith

'This match demonstrated how this team believed they could win from any position. Stumps had to be drawn before they believed they had no chance to win a match.'
– Roger Harper

At Lord's England won a few tight rounds but, to continue in boxing parlance, after staying in the fight for most of the contest, they were mercilessly floored by a late counter-assault to deny them a points decision at the very least.

The second Test was the one match in the series where England were competitive for much of the game, and even threatened a win. A draw seemed their worst-case scenario, which would have meant they avoided a subsequent series whitewash, yet the West Indies made the fifth-highest score ever to win a Test, and without breaking sweat.

When David Gower declared England's second innings half an hour into the final morning to set the tourists a run chase of 342 in 78 overs, few expected what came next. Gordon Greenidge played the innings of his life for 214 not out and Larry Gomes supported him stoically with an unbeaten 92 as Clive Lloyd's team won by nine wickets with 11.5 overs remaining to take a 2-0 lead.

That reference to 'few expected' seemingly did not extend to the West Indies dressing room. They always had the belief they could win from any position. After all, they had proved it before and knew the formula.

Roger Harper recalled an early memory from his time mixing with the West Indies squad, during the first Test against India in Jamaica in 1983. He wasn't playing but still learned a great deal about their team culture. Rain had washed out the fourth day and a draw appeared inevitable. At tea-time on the final day, India were 168/6 and leading by 165. They were comfortable, or so it appeared.

'Our guys were still very much looking at a victory,' remembered Harper. 'They were thinking "a few quick wickets and it's game on". Then after tea, Andy Roberts blew them away by taking the last five wickets very quickly, on a flat Sabina Park pitch.'

Roberts took three wickets in his first over after the interval, to finish with nine in the match. The Windies needed 172 runs on the final evening from just 26 overs. They won with four balls remaining after a scramble to win the game. On that day it was Viv Richards who masterminded the victory with 61 off 36 balls. His first scoring stroke was a six, despite suffering from a painful shoulder.

'That match demonstrated how they believed they could win from any position,' Harper added. 'Stumps had to be drawn before they believed they had no chance to win a match. The approach at Lord's was to go out before lunch, bat to the break and see what happens and take it from there. Then see where we are at tea-time. But right from the start Gordon was able to score freely without having to take huge risks. England were pressing for early wickets and expected the ball to swing around but it never did much at all.'

England began the match in the worst possible way – by losing the toss and being asked to bat first, on the back of their batting failures at Edgbaston. Graeme Fowler had a poor first Test and he now had to prove himself with a new opening partner in Nottinghamshire's Chris Broad, in for the injured Andy Lloyd.

One small mercy was the forced absence of Michael Holding to injury and he was replaced by the Bajan seamer Milton Small, playing his second Test. Clive Lloyd tried to help Small settle into what can either be an intimidating or inspiring atmosphere at Lord's, by asking him to share the new ball with Joel Garner, holding Malcolm Marshall back. That gave the England openers a psychological lift and they were able to post an opening stand of 101, before Broad glanced Marshall off his hip to fall to a spectacular diving catch by Dujon. Fowler was unbeaten on 70 at stumps before going on to his century (106) the next day. Mike Gatting's recall for his former team-mate Derek Randall backfired as he nervously, and over-cautiously, padded up to Marshall in both innings (1 and 29), to be one of his six wickets in the first dig. Another player to endure a miserable recall, after 18 months out of the team, was all-rounder Geoff Miller. He was run out for a duck, but it wasn't any run-out, as Eldine Baptiste spectacularly uprooted his middle stump with a throw from 80 yards on the Warner Stand boundary at long leg.

'As I was attacking the ball, my intention was to run out Downton,' Baptiste recalled, 'but he was running quickly and then I noticed that Miller was quite casual. Malcolm was shouting "keeper's end" because there was nobody to back up behind him, but I wanted Miller and let that thing rip. It went like a bullet to the non-striker's end and was the best ball I ever threw! That's what we practised for. We would mark each other out of ten with throws from the outfield and this was an example of how the preparation paid off.'

The West Indies struggled to cope with Botham's swing initially and collapsed to 35/3 in reply to England's 286. Viv Richards looked in ominous form once again, though, until he was the victim of an awful umpiring error by Barrie Meyer and was lbw to his great friend Botham for 72. Meyer later apologised to Richards and acknowledged he 'may have got that one wrong' – he even considered recalling Richards. Clive Lloyd's patient 39 in three hours at the crease emphasised England's disciplined bowling in helpful conditions.

'In the first innings Botham got the ball to swing around prodigiously,' Harper recalled. 'That created a lot of problems for us even though they were fortunate to get Viv out because that ball was missing another set of stumps.'

Nobody was better than Botham in that era at making the ball talk in the right overcast conditions and he subsequently claimed 8-103. It was the best analysis by an England bowler at home against West Indies, and his second eight-wicket haul at Lord's. The West Indies were indebted to a vital 44 from Baptiste in the lower-middle order. It just about kept the tourists within a sniff of England, conceding a first-innings deficit of only 41 runs.

West Indies came back hard at the home side by reducing them to 36/3 and then 88/4 before Allan Lamb and Botham came together for a vital fifth-wicket stand of 128. That period was the one time in the series when England were on top with the bat and forced Lloyd into setting defensive fields. This was a situation when Lloyd would turn to the ever-reliable seamer Baptiste to keep things tight as regards to the run rate.

'England were going well and Lloydy said to me, "I need a favour from you," Baptiste recalled. "I need you to bowl for the whole session as I want to keep Malcolm and Joel fresh." On that Monday I probably bowled 25 overs on the trot between lunch and after tea and went at less than two runs an over. That was where Lloydy was a great man manager as he came up to me at the end of the day and said, "Because of that long shift you put in, it means England haven't got away from us like they might have done." It felt good to get that praise from the skipper. When we went on to win it made me feel good that I had played my part.'

Lamb went on to his first of three centuries in the series, which was a huge relief to him given that his place in the team was being questioned after his dreadfully poor winter returns and then scores of just 15 and 13 at Edgbaston.

'There were a few doubts about my place I think, but I'm not sure the selectors knew who to stay with and who to drop,' Lamb said. 'One or two writers said they had to stick with me and fortunately they did.'

The Northamptonshire batsman favoured a counter-attacking mentality and prospered by remaining positive, intent on despatching anything short or wayward. Such deliveries were usually rare against this attack, though. Once Botham was out, falling short of a first century against the West Indies, the match took a very interesting twist late on the fourth day when Derek Pringle and Lamb were batting together. The light deteriorated and although the West Indies were still on the back foot in the match the batsmen looked up to the balcony for guidance on whether to come off, and then took matters into their own hands with Gower nowhere to be seen. They opted to came off with 53 minutes of play remaining with the score at 287/7 and with a lead of 328 runs, much to the frustration of the spectators and surprise of the opposition.

West Indies captain Clive Lloyd was relieved England didn't declare on the Monday evening when swing bowling conditions were perfect for Botham. Instead, they declared the following morning in fair conditions, having added just 13 more runs to their score for the loss of two wickets. The day would soon become all about Greenidge, and to a lesser extent Gomes and England's ill-disciplined bowlers.

Broad remembers a very negative outlook when England played the West Indies most of the times he was involved, so the declaration bucked this trend. 'Our aim in those days was to not lose the Test match, rather than have a positive outlook and try to win it. There was very little positivity around.'

The West Indies had scored just ten runs 30 minutes into their run chase, as Bob Willis opened with a tidy enough spell. But England's accuracy and West Indies' cautiousness was soon to change. Gower understandably focused on preventing Greenidge's square cut initially, and successfully, but he was good enough to find other routes to the boundary, through midwicket and long-on. Greenidge plundered 29 boundaries all told.

It wasn't like the English bowlers were not familiar with Greenidge as he had played at Hampshire since 1970. This extensive experience in county cricket made him technically adept and knowledgeable when approaching his innings in England.

'Knowing and understanding the pitches in England would have helped in some way,' he conceded. 'Most counties you played at you were confronted by a different surface. Some pitches you got on were hard but not necessarily fast, others would seam and have pace, green-tops would fizz through. So, all these different surfaces around the country would have different characteristics and it certainly helped my preparations for West Indies tours.

'I tried to develop skills that allowed me to bat well on any kind of surface. Some batsmen roll up and seem to be dampened by the look of certain pitches, but you have to approach all pitches with an open mind. I didn't have the luxury, as an opening batter who faced the first ball throughout my career, of sitting back and learning how the wicket was playing. I had to think on my feet and if I had thought any other way, like becoming negative on pitches that did not look all that easy to bat on, then I don't think I would have survived very long. It's about putting your ability to the test to get the job done.'

This Lord's pitch was clearly to his liking, though in keeping with his philosophy he did assess conditions early on before going about his massacre of the England bowlers. That county experience certainly benefitted Greenidge on three of his four England Test tours: he averaged 65.77 in five Tests in 1976; 81.71 in his five Tests in 1984; and 47 in his four Tests in 1988. Curiously, the only England tour he struggled on was in 1980 when he averaged 20.66 in the five matches that he played. He retired in 1991 having been omitted from West Indies' Test squad for that summer, despite playing in the one-day series.

England were not big on tactics meetings and certainly didn't sit together every night planning ahead for the next day, apart from the team get-together on the night before day one of a Test. 'We sort of chatted, but it was more between the bowlers than as a team,' Lamb said. 'There were no videos to look at in those days; it was a case of make your own arrangements when it came to tactics. Probably over a beer. The bowlers worked it out about where they needed to bowl but there were no team meetings as such like you have nowadays.'

Derek Pringle felt it was difficult anyway to plan for Greenidge because he was such an unpredictable batsman to bowl to. 'You never quite knew what you were going to get with Gordon as on some days he fiddled around a bit and on others he played his shots. On this day he obviously went for it, and everything seemed to find the middle of the bat. He spanked a couple of shots over my head and hit the ball so hard. It was stand and deliver.'

England's only success was that of Desmond Haynes, run out for 17 by Lamb's underarm throw from square leg. That was 57/1 and then 82/1 off 20 overs at lunch. Gower's men needed to take every half-chance if they were going to apply pressure on the West Indies' batsmen, on a flat pitch with no obvious cloud cover to encourage swing. But once Pringle dropped Gomes at first slip it seemed to be a matter of when the West Indies would win rather than if.

Greenidge and Gomes added 132 in 25 overs between lunch and tea, as the opener brought up his hundred off 135 deliveries. Soon after, Botham dropped him (on 110) at slip off Willis. 'If you are going to be forceful you can expect one or two errors to occur,' he admitted. 'That was the way it had to be if you are going to score 340 runs in two and a half sessions. We had to keep up with the rate if we wanted to challenge the target.'

Greenidge maintains his innings was very spontaneous with not too many preconceived plans attached to it. He was especially thankful to his captain, Lloyd, for creating an environment that allowed batsmen like him to go out and express themselves and play freely if they felt that was the best way to bat.

'It really wasn't a planned event. I don't remember us planning to win the game, though we certainly wanted to get as close as possible to our target – and be entertaining. It was a matter of playing each ball and reading the situation and reacting accordingly, as the match moved along. We wanted to stay there or thereabouts with the run rate and we knew, if it ever got to the stage where it became tense, we had sufficient batsmen to see us home or bat out the rest of the overs if we needed to play for the draw. I set myself personal goals and tried to reach those in the timeframe I allowed.'

Greenidge reached his first of two double centuries in the series from 233 deliveries and became the first West Indies player to score a double century in a Lord's Test.

Gomes, meanwhile, was a steadying influence at the other end. The left-handed Trinidadian had played more first-class cricket at Lord's by the end of his career than on any other ground apart from his native Queen's Park Oval in Port of Spain after his previous county stints with Middlesex, so Lord's was a ground that he felt very comfortable on.

The unbroken 287-run partnership between Greenidge and Gomes was a West Indies record against England, surpassing the 249 by Lawrence Rowe and Alvin Kallicharran at Barbados in 1973/74. Greenidge appreciated the role that Gomes played.

'There were many discussions in the middle of the wicket between myself and Larry to see where we were and what we needed to do and how to go about doing it,' said Greenidge, who also revealed that they discussed the matter of whether they should manipulate the scoring as such so that Gomes could reach a second hundred in successive Tests. Gomes, though, chose to just finish the match naturally, whoever was scoring the runs.

With two runs required, Botham switched to off-spin and Gomes immediately scored the winning runs. Botham shared the man of the match award with Greenidge, the first time such an award had ever been split, a decision which irked the West Indies camp. And in fairness to them it was a general custom that the man of the match was from the winning team. Greenidge received all the plaudits then, and still is ...

Paul Downton: 'As soon as Greenidge cut the first ball of the innings for four from Bob Willis who was coming in from the Pavilion End, we all thought, "Shit." It was a bit wide, a bit short and Greenidge absolutely murdered his cut shot. From there, we were always on the defensive.'

Mike Gatting: 'Gordon was a magnificent player and that was as good as I ever saw him play. He didn't slog i – if the ball was there (to hit), he put it away and unfortunately the ball was there quite often. We didn't bowl well but I have a feeling Gordon would have smashed anyone that day. He was incredible.'

Neil Foster: 'In the second innings, Greenidge played amazing, but I remember him getting a top edge off me that went for six. I got none-for in the match, so I was always going to be dropped in those days.'

Roger Harper: 'England thought they could repeat what they had done to us in the first innings again in the second, but the sun came out and the ball didn't swing as much. Gordon Greenidge went to work with Larry Gomes as his co-pilot.'

Jeff Dujon: 'Once Gordon started to open his shoulders, the runs were coming so fast that by the time we reached about a hundred it looked like we could get those runs. That was an exhibition of square cutting like I had never seen before. He was in total control and at his peak. He was just a master technician.'

Paul Terry (who didn't play at Lord's but opened with Greenidge at Hampshire): 'He was always a great player on wickets that did a bit. I remember playing against Surrey and Sylvester Clarke in the early 1980s on a pitch at The Oval that was doing a lot. He left his helmet off and went out in just a sunhat. We all thought, "What the hell is he doing?" because the wicket was up and down. He got hit on the jaw, but he thought playing without a helmet would make him concentrate more. It was a privilege to stand at the non-striker's end to him. We had a few big partnerships and for most of them my share would have been a lot less than his.'

The final word must go to the man himself. We know how he did it, but what happened next?

'We celebrated but not over-celebrated because it was not the end of the tour,' said Greenidge. 'We had a few glasses of champagne or as many as we could afford! Not that they have that problem now – it's by the bottle. We also knew people who lived there and who would cook West Indian food and bring it round to the guys at the hotel.

'We sat together at the hotel having a few drinks and had a whopping big hotel bill when we left!'

Clive Lloyd felt proud that his team had soaked up all of what England had to throw at them and still somehow won the match. 'Winning 5-0 is not something you think about too much,' Lloyd said, 'but once we got past Lord's, I thought, "Maybe it's possible."'

LORD'S SCORECARD
England

	First Innings		Second Innings	
G. Fowler	c Harper b Baptiste	106	lbw b Small	11
B.C. Broad	c Dujon b Marshall	55	c Harper b Garner	0
D.I. Gower	lbw b Marshall	3	c Lloyd b Small	21
A.J. Lamb	lbw b Marshall	23	c Dujon b Marshall	110
M.W. Gatting	lbw b Marshall	1	lbw b Marshall	29
I.T. Botham	c Richards b Baptiste	30	lbw b Garner	81
P.R. Downton	not out	23	lbw b Small	4
G. Miller	run out	0	b Harper	9
D.R. Pringle	lbw b Garner	2	lbw b Garner	8
N.A. Foster	c Harper b Marshall	6	not out	9
R.G.D. Willis	b Marshall	2		
105.5 overs, 35 extras		286	98.3 overs, 18 extras	
			9 wkts dec.	300

Fall of wickets 1st Innings: 1-101 (Broad); 2-106 (Gower); 3-183 (Lamb); 4-185 (Gatting); 5-243 (Fowler); 6-248 (Botham); 7-251 (Miller); 8-255 (Pringle); 9-264 (Foster); 10-286 (Willis)

Bowling: Garner 32-10-67-1; Small 9-0-38-0; Marshall 36.5-10-85-6; Baptiste 20-6-36-2; Harper 8-0-25-0

Fall of wickets 2nd Innings: 1-5 (Broad); 2-33 (Gower); 3-36 (Fowler); 4-88 (Gatting); 5-216 (Botham); 6-230 (Downton); 7-273 (Miller); 8-290 (Lamb); 9-300 (Pringle)

Bowling: Garner 30.3-3-91-3; Small 12-2-40-3; Marshall 22-6-85-2; Baptiste 26-8-48-0; Harper 8-1-18-1.

West Indies

	First Innings		Second Innings	
C.G. Greenidge	c Miller b Botham	1	not out	214
D.L. Haynes	lbw b Botham	12	run out	17
H.A. Gomes	c Gatting b Botham	10	not out	92
I.V.A. Richards	lbw b Botham	72		
C.H. Lloyd	lbw b Botham	39		
P.J. Dujon	c Fowler b Botham	8		
M.D. Marshall	c Pringle b Willis	29		

E.A.E. Baptiste c Downton b Willis 44
R.A. Harper c Gatting b Botham 8
J. Garner c Downton b Botham 6
M.A. Small not out 3
65.4 overs, 13 extras, 245 66.1 overs, 21 extras, 1 wkt
344

Fall of wickets 1st Innings: 1-1 (Greenidge); 2-18 (Haynes); 3-35 (Gomes); 4-138 (Richards); 5-147 (Dujon); 6-173 (Lloyd); 7-213 (Baptiste); 8-231 (Harper); 9-241 (Baptiste); 10-245 (Garner)

Bowling: Willis 19-5-48-2; Botham 27.4-6-103-8; Pringle 11-0-54-0; Foster 6-2-13-0; Miller 2-0-14-0

Fall of wickets 2nd Innings: 1-57 (Haynes)

Bowling: Willis 15-5-48-0; Botham 20.1-2-117-0; Pringle 8-0-44-0; Foster 12-0-69-0; Miller: 11-0-45-0

Toss: West Indies, elected to field first

Player of the match: Gordon Greenidge & Ian Botham (shared)

West Indies won by 9 wickets

Botham and the Final Frontier

'I just couldn't get a hundred against them in the Test arena.'

In a low-key tour game at Worcester in 1991, Ian Botham did what he had always wanted to do – scored a century against the West Indies. And it wasn't your average hundred either, as he blazed 161 from just 139 balls with 134 of those runs in boundaries.

Typical of the man, he wasn't to be outdone by his good friend Viv Richards, who had himself bludgeoned 131 in the first innings of the match. It was enough for Botham to earn a recall into the England team later that summer and play his first Test in two years – the match when he 'couldn't quite get his leg over' and was hit wicket to Curtly Ambrose.

That innings for Worcestershire was brutal and pure theatre, a snapshot of his heyday when such occurrences were not so rare. It was the 36th first-class century of the 38 he made in total. By 1991, he was deep into the back nine of his career and it was, ultimately, a great shame that the time he finally scored three figures against the West Indies it was in such meaningless circumstances. Both the man and the innings deserved better.

Botham took 61 Test wickets against the best team of his generation at an average of 35.18 and scored 792 runs at just 21.40, with a highest of 81 – his excellent cameo at Lord's in '84. Even in one-day internationals his best was just 60.

His rotten luck in captaining England in home and away series against the West Indies at the beginning of his short-lived captaincy tenure was typical of his misfortune against them. Clive Lloyd's team always targeted the opposition's best player and the captain ahead of any other, and here Botham was all-in-one. Subsequently, he made six single-figure scores out of those nine innings.

'I did alright against them with the ball, and I got some vital 60s, 70s and 80s,' Botham said. 'I just couldn't get a hundred against the West Indies in the Test arena, which was frustrating. But believe me I'm not on my own.'

Indeed, he was right in that some very fine batsmen of his time failed to post three figures against the great team, such as Mohammad Azharuddin, Zaheer Abbas and Aravinda de Silva. However, his fierce rivals who were constantly vying with him for the tag of the best all-rounder in the world did manage to conquer that Everest. Kapil Dev managed three hundreds including 100 not out in Port of Spain, Richard Hadlee made 103 in Christchurch in 1980 and Imran Khan scored 123 in Lahore in the same year. It might be pointed out, for fairness, that subcontinental pitches negated the West Indian pace somewhat, but however the stats are presented Botham ultimately fell short in this regard.

'That West Indies team was on another plateau, there was no respite,' commented Botham's long-time Somerset team-mate Vic Marks. 'They were simply on another plane and "Both" was the threat, and they knew it. In fairness to Ian, there weren't too many who did succeed against that lot. There were four of them and they were all bloody good bowlers who were exceptionally quick and gave you nothing.'

If ever an innings deserved better recognition, though, it was the 81 that Botham scored at the home of cricket. It was not just a pulverising display of meaty blows, as most of his longer innings tended to be. It showed how the man, widely known as 'Beefy', could also apply himself when his team needed him as he came to the crease in the second innings with the score on 88/4, so England were effectively 47/4 and the game was in the balance. He added 128 for the fifth wicket with Allan Lamb and they positioned England in such a place whereby David Gower had the luxury of declaring on the fifth morning. He was eventually lbw to his Somerset colleague Joel Garner. Although the logic of the declaration remains open to debate, Botham's effort was generally accepted as one of his more responsible – even underrated – innings that exploited a flat pitch and yet still demonstrated his ability to flay anything wayward.

Team-mate Derek Pringle, one of the many promising England all-rounders to be labelled 'the next Ian Botham' only to fall short of that rather unfair expectation, believes it should not be a surprise that Botham struggled to score the same runs against the West Indies as other nations.

'Ian was a fantastic striker of the ball off the front foot and back, but the West Indies offered far fewer scoring opportunities off the front foot and they bowled much quicker and so there was less room for error,' said Pringle. 'The way he took bowlers on, errors were always going to come but against the West Indies he didn't get away with them. If you attacked them, it might come off for ten minutes, half an hour, but maybe not long enough for you to get a hundred.'

There was a feeling that the West Indies raised their game, if it was even possible, when Botham walked to the crease. Not because they regarded other players any less but because of his destructive nature.

All-rounder Roger Harper acknowledged that the added intelligence from Botham's Somerset team-mates, Richards and Garner, did create a little more of an edge to plans against him.

'Viv and Joel obviously played with him and we all knew and respected his capabilities, that he was a match-winner,' Harper said. 'So, the team always wanted to see the back of him as early as possible. We knew how quickly he scored his runs so that made him dangerous and therefore we were always keen to get rid of him. At times that worked against us as we were a little too attacking against him. But he himself possibly made the same mistake as he wanted to show that he could dominate our bowling attack. In that match at Lord's, he was able to take the attack to our bowlers and get away with it but fell short of the three-figure mark.'

West Indies' plans to negate Botham were understandable. They were not a team to leave things to chance despite their own brilliance. He was, after all, one of the best all-rounders in the world and like his rivals his ball-striking could be devastating when allowed to settle.

West Indies wicketkeeper Jeffrey Dujon revealed that the team met on most nights to discuss tactics for the following day's play and that much of their discussions in the 1984 summer centred around Botham and the importance of limiting his threat.

'We tried to restrict the use of his arms,' Dujon explained. 'He was a big man with a big, heavy bat and we didn't want him swinging through the line too much. We tried to bowl pretty straight to him as well as give him the odd short one, but we were trying to get him out with fuller deliveries, get in the odd yorker.

'He was like Viv, if he sticks around he's going to tear you apart. Ian and Viv were cut from the same cloth – very confident, very determined, and we always looked at him as a threat so we'd spend a bit more time talking about how we were going to bowl to him because he could turn a game in no time.

'We would typically meet the night before and run through who we were playing against, but we mostly discussed how we were going to bowl to them. We had so many guys who played county cricket so our intelligence was good and we knew the various guys we came up against and had a general idea as to where they were strong and where we needed to set our fields.'

Botham threatened to advance towards three figures several times in the 1984 series, and one bowler who frustrated him into giving up his wicket on three occasions was the lesser-paced seamer Eldine Baptiste, who had Botham caught at slip for 30 at Lord's and caught at the wicket for 45 at Headingley.

'I knew what batsmen thought when I came on,' said Baptiste, who often bowled two-hour spells in the nets to perfect his accuracy. 'I wasn't as quick as the others so I'm sure they thought, "This guy is easy." That's why I bowled a tight line and tried to play on the batsman's patience. With Beefy I didn't want him to free his arms and it would frustrate him. He would even say to me out there, "You're not giving me anything to hit!" I'd say, "You got to hit me straight, man." I never liked going for runs and I set myself the target of going for no more than two runs an over. I would wear a batsman down and that's what happened with Beefy.'

The comments from Harper, Dujon and Baptiste reveal as much about the West Indies' professionalism and attention to detail as their enthusiasm to deal with

Botham in the right way, to bring about his downfall. England generally had a team dinner the night before a Test match when they would discuss various plans and tactics and anything beyond that was usually ad hoc and spontaneous. It is more of a trend in recent times that teams meet on most nights to discuss tactics, listen to their analysts' research, watch opposition footage or mark plans down on whiteboards. While the West Indies did not go as far as the current methods, they were still ahead of the game in this regard.

While the West Indies certainly targeted Botham, it could be argued that he did not always do himself justice either. He struggled to play the long game when required. Take the mercurial Ben Stokes from recent times. He is not any more destructive than Botham was but, perhaps, he has proven to be a more astute chess player when he has needed to sit in at the start of innings before opening his shoulders. Stokes, for instance, soaked up 73 balls for just three runs at the start of his incredible match-winning 135 not out against Australia in 2019. It would have been unusual to see Botham play that type of cautious innings.

Vic Marks believes ego was at play in much of Botham's good and bad performances. It helped him to produce the unthinkable and magical but had a negative aspect too. Especially, Marks suggested, when he was playing against Richards. The competitive nature in Botham encouraged him to outdo his friend, whether for Somerset or England when playing against the West Indies.

'Both was the master of all, but he wasn't the master of Viv,' Marks said. 'Neither of them would say this, I imagine, but when they had partnerships together Viv would let Ian have his head, whereas Ian would try to outhit Viv and it would often lead to his downfall. That was just his competitive spirit, which came naturally.

'Both was also heavily scarred from that first tour as captain (to the Caribbean in 1980/81). They really went after him. When he came back from that tour, we played Lancashire at Old Trafford early season and, watching Michael Holding bowling quickly side-on from the old dressing rooms, he said, "I won't get a run here," which was probably the only time I can ever remember him doubting himself or showing a lack of that self-belief that defined him.' Botham was caught off Holding for a duck, though he later took four wickets to help Somerset win the match.)

Sometimes the very presence of a genius in your team can create a subconscious complacency on the part of the other members. Botham's name is synonymous with the Ashes series in 1981 because of the miraculous displays he was able to achieve with bat *and* ball.

Ideally, one would like to think at Test match level each individual is striving to exploit every ounce of their ability. Surely 99 per cent of the time that is the case? However, it would only be natural or understandable that if you have a Brian Lara in your side, or a Donald Bradman, a Shane Warne or, in this case, an Ian Botham, team members might occasionally allow themselves to think at a time when their own confidence is low, "Well, if I don't score the runs today, Brian will or Viv will or we'll be fine, Warney will clean them up." The only problem is that even geniuses can fail or be inconsistent, as was the case with Botham in 1984 and at other stages against the West Indies.

'If you have got Ian Botham on your side as an acknowledged great all-rounder, you are hoping for great things,' David Gower admitted. 'But if they don't happen, they don't happen.

'He could bat, of course he could. Beefy made lots of runs in the Ashes and that gave him the stage to become a superstar after years like 1981. If I said the West Indies targeted him, it overlooks the fact they targeted everyone. But he was our totem and maybe because of who he was and because of his friendship with Viv they subconsciously tried that bit harder against him.'

Gatting's Woe and Fowler's Glow

'I was desperate for runs and was worrying too much
about not getting out instead of playing each ball
on its merits. The head is a funny thing at times.' –
Mike Gatting

It was at the MA Chidambaram Stadium, Chepauk in Madras (now Chennai) where Graeme Fowler (201) and Mike Gatting (207) became the first pair to score double centuries in the same innings of a Test match for England. Not wishing to undermine their match-winning, series-defining record second-wicket partnership of 241, but India's defensive fields, dropped chances and lack of pace certainly helped their cause. The situation was very different just over six months earlier, when they came together at Lord's against the West Indies. It would be akin to being transformed from a pleasant stroll by a tranquil river on a summer's day to falling into white-water rapids laced with boulders and steep waterfalls.

Fowler spent the night before the Lord's Test wracked with anxiety after he had managed scores of 0 and 7 in the first Test, when he had been caught behind and lbw to Joel Garner, at least proud in the knowledge he had twice fallen to the best bowler on show. Fowler also had the anguish of losing his opening partner Andy Lloyd to the sickening blow on his temple that would subsequently end his Test career. So, it was little surprise then that Fowler, widely known as 'Foxy', was having trouble sleeping on the night of Wednesday, 27 June. Not even the memory of scoring 94 in a 55-over tour match against the West Indians at Liverpool a month earlier could settle him.

To ease his racing mind, he called room service at 1am and ordered three pints of Guinness. It did the trick, calmed him enough to have a good night's sleep and he finished the following day 70 not out after Clive Lloyd had won the toss and put England in. Fowler, who combined in an opening stand of 101 with Test debutant Chris Broad, took his score on to 106 on day two, courtesy of a slog-sleep off Roger Harper to go to 99 before registering what would become the second of three Test hundreds in his career. After day one Fowler had repeated his tried and tested late-night formula of a trio of pints. He needed it, having had his box split in two by a quick delivery from Garner to leave him with 'sore bollocks' for the rest of the day. It would be the innings that he could be most proud of once retired. Yes, he scored more in Madras in a winning cause, but to reach three figures against this West Indies team really meant something. It occurred in a losing cause, but he knew he had earned the respect of the most fearsome bowling attack of the era, even though Michael Holding was absent through injury.

Fowler's personal glory was a far cry from the miserable experience that Gatting had at Lord's. It was a significant match for the Middlesex batsman playing on his home ground, for he had been omitted for the first Test and only won a recall after Derek Randall was dropped, for good. Gatting had an average winter in New Zealand and Pakistan, though 75 and 53 in Pakistan looked good enough in the scorebook but clearly not for the ruthless selectors. He played against the West Indies in the first two Texaco Trophy matches but fell cheaply for 0 and 6 to Garner on both occasions and was dropped for the deciding game at Lord's.

A week before Randall was terrorised in his final Test at Edgbaston, though, Gatting was busy constructing a career-best score of 258 against Somerset at Bath and it was enough to convince the selectors he deserved another chance, but only after first choice Martyn Moxon was forced to withdraw from the squad.

'I was in a poor period, in and out of the (England) team,' Gatting reflected. 'Although I had been around since my debut in 1978, I didn't really get my head around Test cricket and I can't blame anyone else but me. I probably didn't expect to start the series against the West Indies because I'd had a couple of poor series. Those were the days when you never expected to be selected if you hadn't been playing well. That was the reality then. It just got you more fired up to get back in as quick as you could.'

Lord's was the one match in the Test series where England were mostly competitive, especially with the bat. As well as Fowler's century, Lamb added a hundred in the second innings, while Chris Broad made a promising 55 in his first match and Ian Botham flayed the West Indies for 81. Sadly for Gatting, runs were hard to come by and he never played again in the series. Here, he was lbw to Marshall for 1 and then 29.

'I padded up to Malcolm twice, because it was the time of day when you didn't want to get out,' Gatting recalled. 'I was thinking too much about leaving the ball instead of playing the ball and this is a stupid thought pattern you get into when things aren't going for you. I was desperate for runs and was worrying too much about not getting out instead of playing each ball on its merits. The head is a funny thing at times. When you know you haven't got runs against them you can start thinking quite negatively.'

It will not provide any solace to Gatting, but his two lbws contributed to a joint record 12 such dismissals in the match, equalling the Dunedin Test in 1979/80 between New Zealand and West Indies. Gatting padding up in the second innings to a ball coming back off the Lord's slope, a ground he knew well, was symptomatic of his cluttered thinking then.

Gower had some sympathy for Gatting as did all the England batsmen who understood the gravity of the challenge facing all of them.

'Malcolm was a bloody good bowler and Mike clearly thought, "Stick the pad out to that, that will be a good leave, oh wait, it's swinging back in, oh dear." Easily done. It's perfectly understandable why Mike had problems against him because he was a damn good bowler.'

The match summed up Gatting's fortunes as far as the West Indies went. Even on tour in the Caribbean, 18 months later, he was in good form before a Marshall bouncer broke his nose and ruled him out until the final match.

And in the 1981 series, he had expected to play more after scoring 94 against the West Indies Cricket Board's President's XI, but instead sat on the sidelines and lost form. By the time he was recalled for the third Test at Barbados, skipper Ian Botham asked him to bat at three. He scored 2 and 0 and faced just three balls in the match, out to Andy Roberts and then Michael Holding, who bowled that infamously hostile spell to Geoffrey Boycott in the same game.

That Gatting averaged just 15 against the West Indies in 17 innings suggests he had serious deficiencies against pace bowling. He was renowned as a better player of spin but still, in county cricket he scored significant runs against Joel Garner, Colin Croft and Sylvester Clarke. Just not when they all played together:

1979, 93 not out v Somerset and Joel Garner at Lord's

1980, 136 v Surrey and Sylvester Clarke at Lord's

1983, 106 v Somerset and Joel Garner at Lord's

1982, 192 v Surrey and Sylvester Clarke at The Oval

1982, 133 not out v Lancashire and Colin Croft at Lord's

Who would have foreseen such travails in Test cricket for Gatting when he scored a brilliant 128 for England under-19s in 1976 against his West Indian counterparts who included a rookie Malcolm Marshall, two years before they both made their Test debuts?

In that 40-over one-day international at Guaracara Park in Trinidad, the England team contained six players who would go on to represent their country at either Test or ODI level, yet Gatting appeared the most assured of them all at this stage, alongside Gower, Bill Athey and Chris Cowdrey. He came in at number five with his team precariously placed on 32/3 and helped them to a winning score of 280.

Gatting himself is still a little confused by the statistic and especially because he knows he scored plenty of runs against pace bowling at different junctures. It says much about the pressure this West Indies team applied, even against experienced players like Gatting.

'I can only assume I had issues with the technical side of my game as well as the mental aspect,' he acknowledged. 'Or perhaps I was trying too hard.'

Gatting had to rely on Gower's backing in a selection meeting to make the triumphant tour to India in 1984/85. Gower claims he used up his 'captaincy vote cards' with Gatting and spinner Phil Edmonds and subsequently acceded to other selections he probably was less passionate about. He felt sorry for how Gatting had been harshly dropped in the West Indies series but did not believe there was much he could do to prevent his axing which came just six weeks into his England captaincy career.

'Maybe it was tough on Mike that he was dropped after one Test, but I was yet to develop enough confidence to fight the selectors every time they wanted to drop someone,' Gower reasoned. 'I didn't sit there meekly and take everything they said. I put forward my own opinions, but after having your own input you have to give a bit of ground to win other selectorial battles at other times. They will let you win some and they will want to win others.'

The story of Chris Broad's Lord's debut was much happier, after he learned of his call-up from Gower at a John Player League Sunday match between Notts and Leicestershire days prior to the Test.

'The selectors had this theory that the West Indies fast bowlers didn't bowl as well to left-handers,' said Broad. 'That theory was very prevalent at the time and maybe that was why other openers were not selected ahead of me (such as Tim Robinson, Kim Barnett, Chris Smith, Paul Terry, Chris Tavare or Peter Roebuck). Fowler was already there and I was replacing another left-hander, Andy Lloyd. I may not have had the best of starts as far as hundreds were concerned but there is more to batting than just getting hundreds, though that is obviously important. My guess is the selectors saw something in me from my days at Gloucestershire that told them I had a good technique against fast bowling.'

Once Broad reached Lord's he was greeted by England batting legend and chairman of selectors Peter May, who advised him, 'Here's your cap and sweaters … you have two Tests to show us what you can do.'

The tall left-hander had developed a reputation at Gloucestershire and then Notts as someone who stood up well to fast bowling, with a reliable, almost mechanical, straight bat technique. He faced Glamorgan overseas quick Winston Davis two weeks earlier and scored 57 at Trent Bridge. Davis was subsequently drafted into West Indies' tour party.

Broad had experience of batting against Marshall and Hampshire in 1981, '82 and '83; he'd scored 65 against Somerset and Garner at Bristol in 1982 and 97 against Eldine Baptiste and Kent at Folkestone in the same year, so the signs were positive. He hadn't faced as much of Michael Holding but that was not an immediate problem with the bowler absent from Lord's. He showed he was comfortable against him, though, when scoring 171 for Notts at Derbyshire the following year, albeit when Holding was a little slower than in his heyday.

Broad's 55 and a second-innings duck represented a solid if not spectacular Test debut. He struck five boundaries in 12 deliveries at one stage, to demonstrate his capability of despatching the loose ball when given the opportunity.

'It helped that there was a lot of inclement weather around and we went off for bad light a few times, which meant their bowlers couldn't get any decent rhythm going,' Broad recalled. 'West Indies opening the bowling with Milton Small ahead of Malcolm Marshall was also a blessing.

'I needed that bit of good fortune because I was in the changing room at the time of the toss and became very nervous when it was announced we'd be batting first. I was signing a few team sheets and suddenly I struggled to write my name!'

The Declaration

'We shouldn't have declared, there was no point in it. I think Gower was pressured into that decision. We were never going to win so there was no value in declaring.' – Neil Foster

David Gower became the first England captain since Norman Yardley in 1948 to declare a second innings and lose. But that piece of history was not simply attributable to the decision itself and the subsequent brilliance of Gordon Greenidge's double century.

England's decision to come off for bad light the night before had a significant bearing on the success of the declaration, or lack of it. Normally a good or bad declaration would leave a small mark on history, but this one gained notoriety when it led to a series whitewash – West Indies' first such result over England.

In brief, England were in the rare situation of coasting against a West Indies bowling attack as Allan Lamb reached 109 and all-rounder Derek Pringle was on 6. England were 287/7 at the time and leading by 328 runs.

There were 53 minutes of play left on the Monday, the fourth evening, when the light worsened over St John's Wood, with West Indian backs against the wall. But

England took the light, a decision West Indies bowler Joel Garner referred to as being surprising and absurd.

The batsmen's recollections are contrasting but the one common theme is that neither wanted to come off. As the senior partner, Lamb felt the need to look towards the captain for the final say. However, Gower and his teammates were nowhere to be seen on the balcony. Gower was engrossed in the BBC's coverage of Wimbledon being shown on the dressing room TV. So, Lamb made an executive decision and came off.

'I said to Lamby, "We're on top here, we'd look stupid if we go off,"' recalled Pringle. 'I didn't see what we had to gain by going off. He thought the captain should make that decision and of course David was nowhere to be seen as he was watching Wimbledon.'

Lamb's account is similar but with a few slight differences.

'Pring came into bat, and he was struggling to see the ball. I was fine and thought the light was still good, but he was struggling. I then said to the umpires, "Pring is struggling with the light, we are going to have to come off." They got their light meters out and offered us the chance to go off. I looked up to the dressing room balcony for some guidance but there was nobody there. So we went off to a chorus of boos from the Lord's crowd. 'When we walked into the dressing room, they were watching Wimbledon and someone said, "What you guys doing here?" I told them we came in for bad light.'

The media reaction was one of shock and surprise. On the BBC's *Test Match Special* summariser Trevor Bailey said the batsmen "would be simply mad" to go off. John Woodcock wrote in *The Times*: 'Lamb had batted for over six hours, so to lead Pringle off was his first mistake.' The crowd and media were unanimous in their condemnation of the decision, at a rare time when the West Indies were on the defensive.

'I don't think there was anything wrong with the declaration the following morning as there was no way Bob Willis was going to hang around too long with the speed Malcolm was bowling that morning,' Eldine Baptiste reasoned. 'But what hurt England was them taking the light on the previous evening. That was the difference between them and us. If we smelt blood, we would be ultra-aggressive and finish a team off. They were more conservative, and it showed in both teams' mentalities.'

Paul Downton agreed with his former Kent team-mate. 'It was getting a bit dark, but I think that decision to take the light reflected our lack of confidence as a side more than anything,' Downton said. 'If you looked at us man for man you knew we weren't the best side on the field so we subconsciously took quite a negative attitude into the series. If we had been a more confident team, I'm sure we would have batted on and built on our ascendency. The ability to go for the jugular and grab a bigger lead just didn't seem to be there. We played with fear – our mindset wasn't positive enough at the time and, in the end, it became more about preserving what we had than improving our position.'

Clive Lloyd was pleased that England didn't declare on that Monday evening, fearing the overcast conditions might encourage the swing that Ian Botham was able to generate in the first innings with his 8-103.

Instead, England resumed on Tuesday's final morning in much more clement batting conditions. They 'faffed around', according to Pringle, for a further 13 runs for two more wickets when Gower called in Neil Foster on the fall of Pringle's wicket, meaning Bob Willis did not have to bat. Foster was 9 not out from just four balls, having struck two boundaries.

West Indies were set 342 in 78 overs, or five and a half hours, and subsequently won with 11.5 overs remaining.

'We shouldn't have declared, there was no point in that,' Foster said, still with a hint of disbelief in his voice 40 years later. 'I think Gower was pressured into that decision. We were never going to win so there was no value in declaring. We always came second against the West Indies in those days but for once we had a situation where we got our noses in front and, at the very least, we shouldn't have lost the game when you consider the few overs remaining and the rate they had to score at.

'We may as well have carried on batting for as long as possible, took more time out of the match and tried to come out with an honourable draw. We might have been bowled out in two balls, but we may also have kept them out for another 20 or 30 minutes which could have made a difference to the way Greenidge approached things. David might have wanted to make his mark as a new captain.'

It obviously backfired on Gower and he is not the only captain to make a poor declaration in hindsight. Stand-in skipper Adam Gilchrist allowed England and Mark

Butcher the opportunity to chase down an unlikely target and win in 2001 at Headingley. Ironically, that decision prevented a whitewash rather than led to one, as England slid to a 4-1 series loss that summer.

It also happened in reverse in 1968 when the attack-minded West Indies captain Garfield Sobers declared to leave England 215 to win, which they managed to achieve. Sobers was lambasted in parts of the Caribbean and they didn't let him forget it for many years. Gower did not receive much of the same because there was a resignation that 5-0 in no way flattered the West Indies in 1984.

'We weren't in any way worried about getting bowled out on that final day at Lord's,' Jeffrey Dujon recalled, 'but nobody could have expected what Gordon went on to produce. The pitch was flat, so I didn't see us getting bowled out again on that as even we toiled quite a bit in England's second innings.'

Gower had faced an awkward dilemma on that Tuesday morning as various opinions came his way, some to bat on, some to declare.

'(Chairman of selectors) Peter May told David to declare overnight,' said Lamb. 'When I heard this, I said, "David, it's the flattest wicket I have ever played on. You can't declare."'

Middlesex captain Mike Gatting knew Lord's better than anyone on either team, as he played his county cricket there. He was also in Gower's ear. 'We were batting through to the end and going nowhere, and I said, "David, they're not going to get 350 in 60-odd overs, so why don't we just put them in, try to take a few wickets and gain some kind of psychological advantage before the next Test." David said, "That's not a bad shout." So, we declared.'

These are times when captains need to stay strong-minded, listen to the views of those they respect and then make his, or her, own decision based on instinct with the benefit of all the facts and conditions. In fairness to Gower, he would not have reckoned on no swing, a Greenidge masterclass and a horrendous day at the office for *all* the bowlers at his disposal.

So, what did the captain himself make of everything?

'In the first instance, I didn't really have a problem with coming off for bad light at that stage,' Gower reflected. 'From the comfort of the commentary box, it's easy for those guys to say they should have carried on. That didn't worry me. The more interesting thing to me is the following morning where Peter May was telling me that we should declare early. It was the most glorious day with the sun out, the pitch had no demons in it, though maybe it behaved differently in the gloom. It looked like a good batting day so my reply to Peter was, "I'm not so sure, look at the weather, the pitch, it's all pointing to good batting conditions."

'I was also mindful of that batting line-up: Greenidge, Haynes, Richards et cetera. Yes, Lamby would also have given me his opinion as a friend and an ally so I had all sorts of theories of what I should do but, ultimately, I had to make that decision. I chose to bat on a bit longer and eventually called them in, leaving them 342 to win.

'If you had analysts in those days and crunched the numbers 342 runs to get with an hour before lunch and two sessions after, what's the worst that can happen? Something special had to happen for them to win. And it fucking well did.'

England's Bowlers 'Threw in the Towel'

'There was no swing, no spin, we didn't have anything to defend ourselves with and it felt like we were left naked against the onslaught of Greenidge.' – Neil Foster

The final day of the second Test might best be summarised in a bullet point presentation of three main aspects:

- England declared when they did not need to, whatever difference it 'might' have made. 'Possibly' an extra 20 or 30 minutes taken out of their innings 'could' have forced a less aggressive approach from the tourists. 'Maybe'.

- England bowled without discipline: the wrong lengths, the wrong lines, dropped chances (Larry Gomes was dropped early by Derek Pringle, and Ian Botham dropped Greenidge on 110), and they ultimately had no control of the West Indies run rate.

- *Willis: 15-5-48-0; Botham 20.1-2-117-0; Pringle 8-0-44-0; Foster 12-0-69-0; Miller 11-0-45-0.*

- Greenidge played the innings of his life with a scintillating double century (214*) and was supported wonderfully by Gomes (92*).

All the above are true. However, the key point is fact number 2 because if fact 2 had a different origin such as

England bowled with discipline, accuracy, intelligence and fielded reliably well then fact 1 probably becomes irrelevant in a tame draw and fact 3 might still have been the case but with a less damaging outcome for England.

Had Greenidge scored an unbeaten 130 in a bore draw it would not have been remembered with anywhere near the same reverence as his match-winning innings. It is regarded as one of the best Test match innings, at least at Lord's, but again things could have been so very different with a better bowling display from England.

'We bowled like absolute moles, we really did,' Mike Gatting admitted. 'Gordon played unbelievably well though while the sun was out. But we did help him quite a bit.'

There is not an England player from the match whose recollection from that sunny fifth day's play is anything but one of disappointment at how they allowed a strong position to disintegrate from what was seemingly an unlikely defeat at the start of the day, never mind an eventual series whitewash.

Even West Indies' spearhead Malcolm Marshall was surprised at how lacklustre England's bowling was. He was clear in his conclusion as to where England lost that Test match.

'The England batsmen had done all that could have been asked of them,' Marshall commented, 'but the frailty of their bowling let them down again (after the first Test). Despite having faced Greenidge in county cricket for many years, Willis, Botham, Pringle, Foster and Miller fed his strengths outside the off stump.

'England threw in the towel. The selectors could have made as many changes as they liked for the third Test, but it would have made no difference because the players had given up.'

In hindsight, if they were being brutally honest, every England player from that series would admit to being in possession of an inferiority complex throughout that Test series – even eternal optimist Ian Botham. And understandably so. Still, they would have wanted to compete and earn the respect of their opponents. So, to hear Marshall's cutting but honest observations would be hurtful.

Players are never guaranteed to take wickets or score runs but the least they can expect of themselves is to compete and fight hard for their country. To be accused of doing the opposite and throwing in the towel as early as the second Test, wow, that would have bruised a few egos.

So what happened? How did it transpire that way on day five?

Clearly, conditions were very different to how they were on the first three days of the match when the ball swung around, especially for Botham, who bowled skilfully for his 8-103. Allan Lamb detected the change in conditions, for the better, when he was plundering his first of three hundreds in the series on day four.

'I sort of knew they were going to get the runs because the wicket was so flat,' Lamb said. 'We knew the best place to bowl to them was just short of a length on or around off stump, and try to have them nick off to slip, but it didn't work out that way most of the time.'

Seamer Derek Pringle added, 'We were lulled a bit because in the first innings Botham bowled brilliantly and swung the ball around, and you would expect later in the match there would be cracks or some variation in bounce but, when they went out to chase, that pitch was dead as a dodo.

'Botham kept saying to David (Gower), "Give me one more over and I'll get a wicket," and this went on for almost an hour. He ended up going at six an over! English Test pitches generally in those days were flat. Only Headingley gave you something to work with in terms of seam movement. My old Essex team-mate Mark Waugh used to tell me that the best Test pitches to bat on in the world are in England. It certainly looked like it at Lord's that day.'

Captain Gower looks back ruefully, still. He has made peace more with his decision to declare than the fact his bowlers let him and the team down. At the tea interval Gower showed a nastier side to his normally laconic style of leadership after trying unsuccessfully to execute wicket-taking plans all day.

'Your first aim as a captain is to exude calm and confidence, pretend to be confident with your decision-making, be confident with how you handle your team, and try not to lose it when things aren't going your way,' explained Gower.

'Every now and again, a ten-minute rant is something you can use to rouse people from lethargy, casualness or whatever, before you go back to being calm and considered again. I didn't do that very often but, after a shit afternoon,

I felt it was needed. They were still one wicket down, cruising to victory and it looked like the game was gone.'

He added: 'When we ran out (Desmond) Haynes, we thought, "Okay, here we go. We're on a roll now." But Greenidge's innings was spectacular, and he was supported superbly by Gomes, who was underrated. We didn't bowl very well, though. I packed the off side, trying to limit them, then Beefy or someone else would bowl too straight and Gomes would nudge it down the hill through fine leg for four. It was very frustrating. To lose with 12 overs to go at the end of the day was just horrible. It was a brutal day.'

Don Topley was England's 12th man, fielding for the injured Chris Broad, and he said he will never forget the disconsolation in the dressing room after the match.

'I remember before we went out on the final day, they were genuinely optimistic that they could put the West Indies under pressure. And when they got back to the dressing room a couple of sessions later it was a very forlorn atmosphere.'

For his eight-wicket haul in the first innings and second-innings 81, Botham surprisingly shared the man of the match award with Greenidge; not that Botham was in any mood to delight at his award.

It's tough to deny Botham performed way below his usual standards in the second innings, but in a way that was a snapshot of the rough England occasionally had to accept with his smooth. He over-attacked with his lengths, became comfortable to pick off and over-coerced Gower into bowling him more than he deserved. Botham had an infectious ability to want to be the man who got his team over the line and it would have been difficult for any skipper to suppress that confidence by denying him the stage.

'He didn't like to be sidelined,' said Gatting, who led Botham on the successful Ashes tour in 1986/87. 'That's just Beefy's nature, and he really did push David to let him bowl, probably wrongly. But that was Beefy, who always wanted to be in the game.'

Another one of those bowlers in the dock, Neil Foster, admitted to feeling miffed by the declaration in the first instance, yet wasn't trying to excuse how he and his fellow bowlers performed in the event.

'It wasn't a declaration that felt like it favoured us,' Foster reflected. 'We should have kept them out in the field for as long as possible. There was no swing, no spin, we didn't have anything to defend ourselves with and it felt like we were left naked against the onslaught of Greenidge.

'But in saying that, we got a bit giddy trying to bowl them out and sprayed it all over the place. They subsequently got off to a flier on a good wicket and Greenidge played amazingly.'

Foster was dropped after this match, as was Miller, but Willis, Botham and Pringle were retained for Headingley. Foster was not surprised to have endured a bad match and be dropped.

'Botham was still our focal point and pretty much guaranteed to be in the side, but everyone else were fighting amongst themselves,' Foster said. 'If we had a good game, we might get another one. If not, we made changes, with no phone call, no explanation, no encouragement.'

As Chris Broad said, the fact their sole wicket was a run-out summed up the level of toil required just to buy a wicket.

But when chances did come England were off their game and unable to take them. Who knows if the early departure of Gomes, or dismissing Greenidge for a hundred runs less than he ended up with, would have made any difference?

'I was a bit slow to move,' Pringle said of his effort to catch Gomes at first slip. 'I thought at first it was Beefy's catch (at second slip), and he probably thought it was my catch.'

That just about summed up England's day.

The Twelfth Man Who Stole the Show

'It probably took the best part of 30 years for me to come to terms with the end of my county career and get over that disappointment. When I look back at my career, I see there were mental health issues I needed help with, but that kind of support just wasn't there like it is now. You had to get on with it.' – Julian Wyatt

Don Topley left the Hyelm Hostel in Hampstead on the morning of Saturday, 30 June 1984 as just another ambitious cricket wannabe on the prestigious MCC Young Cricketers' programme. Little did he know his career would take a strange but pleasant twist that day. A twist that he would be frequently associated with for the rest of his life.

On his way to Lord's, he stopped to call his father Tom
– a retired naval officer – from a pay phone to check in and
describe how his day was looking. 'I'll be selling scorecards
this morning, Dad, and I might be on covers duty this
afternoon,' said young 'Toppers' as he was known to
everyone at Lord's. His afternoon may well have included a
sneaky trip to the local pub in nearby Regents Park, which
wasn't an unusual excursion for some of the groundstaff
when the weather could be trusted to remain fine.

Tom Topley loved his cricket, and his routine was to
complete his shopping trip in the morning and then settle
down in front of the television at home to watch the Test
match; in this instance the third day of the second Test
between England and West Indies at Lord's.

Imagine Tom's surprise then when his boy came
running down the steps of the famous old Lord's pavilion
in full whites to field for England! All this happening live
on the BBC's television coverage being broadcast to the
nation. 'Dad thought he was seeing things,' laughed Don,
recalling the day.

How did it get to this? What the hell happened for a
scorecard seller who had never played a first-class match
in his life to suddenly become England's emergency fielder
for the rest of the Test, from Saturday morning through
to Tuesday afternoon?

Sussex batsman Paul Parker was the designated 12th
man, but he was ill so Don Wilson, in charge of MCC
Young Cricketers, dashed to the scorecard hut at the
Grace Gates, dressed in his England blazer and whites
and with cigarette in hand, found Topley and said in front

of everyone, 'Toppers! What are you doing here? Your country needs you. I've had Peter May on to me; they're a man down and need my best fielder straight away and that is you, Toppers. Hurry up and get to the England dressing room, now!'

'I had a shirt and tie on and an MCC blazer and was perplexed and immediately thought it was a stitch-up,' remembered Topley. 'I wasn't in a position to argue with Wils, so I had no choice but to go along with it all.

'I dashed over to where my whites were behind the Nursery Ground and discovered they were filthy dirty. I thought I can't go on and field for England in those. I went to see Gordon Jenkins in the Lord's Shop and persuaded him to lend me a pair of trousers after telling him I was about to field for England! Finally, after dashing here, there and everywhere, I arrived at the door of the England dressing room and was still thinking it was a wind-up and I half-expected Jeremy Beadle to jump out of some door as he often did on that famous TV show he used to host (*Beadle's About*).

'I gave the dressing room door a gentle knock and the attendant opened the door, closely followed by Peter May, who said, "Are you Toppers? Hurry up son, you're going out to field now." Only then did it dawn on me that this was real.'

And the story didn't end with a mere appearance. Topley scrambled down to the Long Room, where he frantically laced his boots up. The 'who's that guy' murmurings all around him were not discreet. But before Topley had time to feel insecure or think about what was going on, the injured Broad was walking past him, saying, 'You're on.' And off he went, down to fine leg to field to Bob Willis.

'Literally within five minutes of being on the field,' said Topley, 'Malcolm Marshall hooked a bouncer to me, and I was taking this fantastic one-handed catch on the boundary with my left hand. The crowd erupted, but I knew straight away I had trod on the rope and there was no way I was getting away with it. There were lots of West Indian stewards on the boundary shouting, "That's not out maan, you stepped on the rope!"

'Bob Willis didn't exactly give me a bollocking, but he critiqued me, asking why I didn't throw it in the air and catch it after stepping back on to the field. It was a wonderful idea from Bob, but nobody did that kind of fielding then. Probably not for another 30 years. I was too junior to say anything back to Bob, but I was tempted to say, "Bloody hell mate, give me a break, I was a nobody selling scorecards ten minutes ago!"

'It was a crazy situation as I never even had a county contract and was just an apprentice cricketer on the Lord's staff.'

While Topley couldn't claim the catch officially, the moment still became embedded in English cricket folklore, and he would always be synonymous with it thereafter.

He also remembers fielding at bat-pad on the off side to the dominant Gordon Greenidge for a while with no box, shin pads or helmet. Thankfully, no injury occurred to overshadow his 'catch'.

In the off-season leading in to the 1984 summer Topley worked for logistics company Charles Kendall & Partners as a purchasing clerk for the Sultan of Oman. He only did it for six months before telling them he was going to try and become a professional cricketer. His ambition did not prove to be fruitless.

His Lord's fielding experience with England never showcased the bowling ability he would later exhibit in a ten-year career with Essex, but it certainly gave him a glimpse of fame and the big-match atmosphere.

He made his first-class debut the following season in a one-off game for Surrey, before signing for Essex and becoming an important member of a successful county team along with the likes of Graham Gooch, Derek Pringle, Neil Foster, a young Nasser Hussain and, from 1987, Geoff Miller, who Topley regarded as the friendliest to him during his England duty.

Miller, who would later become Topley's roommate at Essex, gifted Topley his old England coffin with 'England Tour to Australia & New Zealand 1982-83' on. He still has it in his Suffolk home and uses it to keep his collection of football match programmes in.

Topley's surreal fielding moment, on a surreal day in a match that also included a surreal ending courtesy of Gordon Greenidge, had other surreal moments to accompany it.

Don Wilson used to host a garden party after a Test match Saturday for the great and the good, according to Topley, as he lived in the flat above the old MCC Shop. Anyone from Garry Sobers, Denis Compton and Fred

Trueman to other famous names that had been to Lord's that day could be present. The MCC Young Cricketers would go along and serve drinks and later have their own party.

'When I left the pavilion still dressed in my whites to go to Wils's party, the first person I bumped into was Colin Cowdrey, who was a family friend as my brother, Peter, played with him at Kent,' said Topley.

'He was such a lovely man. "Donald," he said, "what a day you've had and such a wonderful catch. Bad luck with that, old boy." As we walked round to Wils's soirée together, I was stopped for my autograph by what felt like thousands of people as they left the ground.

'It was terribly embarrassing that Colin, this legend of the game with 114 Test matches and over 7,000 runs, was standing there in his suit and tie, barely noticed, while I signed these autographs, and nobody asked for his. It must have taken us 45 minutes to walk around the ground to Wils's party and Colin was so gracious and patient as he walked with me.'

Topley was back at Lord's later that summer when England requested him to be their official 12th man for the one-off Test match against Sri Lanka. On that occasion there were no one-handed catches or autograph melees.

West Indies legends Desmond Haynes and Gordon Greenidge became friends of Topley in later years and would still tease him that he made an easy catch look difficult.

Topley's first official catch in first-class cricket, incidentally, came on his debut in 1985 against Cambridge

University, when he caught little-known Maharaj Ahluwalia off the bowling of off-spinner Chris Bullen. The 'catch that wasn't', though, will remain a greater part of his legacy.

'I was trying to make a career for myself at that time and after subsequently spending ten years with Essex I like to think I did okay and I'm proud of my record (367 wickets at an average of 27.64),' Topley said.

'It's funny that I'm probably still best remembered for that catch at Lord's. I made some good contributions towards Essex's success as we were one of the best county teams in history.

'But I'm realistic enough to acknowledge I reached my ceiling and was essentially a journeyman,' but with a very interesting back story!

... and a West Country Rookie

Julian Wyatt was approaching his 21st birthday when his native Somerset hosted the touring West Indians in May 1984. He relished the challenge of taking on the best cricket team in the world with a boyish enthusiasm, despite the prospect of facing the new ball against the great Malcolm Marshall.

We know now he was the standout performer for Somerset, top-scoring in both innings on a spiteful pitch that saw two of his team-mates badly injured. Nigel Popplewell was hit on the side of the helmet by a short Marshall off-cutter that seamed back sharply, while Mark Davis was also hit by Marshall and was absent hurt for the remainder of the match.

Wyatt's maturity to withstand the pace of Marshall in particular, as well as Milton Small, Courtney Walsh and off-spinner Roger Harper impressed, though both innings ultimately stand as highlights of what later became an unfulfilled career.

'Jules batted really well and was very brave against an attack that was up for the challenge given places were all to play for ahead of the Test series,' said Vic Marks, stand-in captain in the match. 'The strange thing was that while Jules could be brilliant against quality fast bowling, as was the case in this match on a lively early-season pitch, he was also a sucker for nicking off to second slip off a medium-paced outswinger.'

Wyatt had registered his maiden first-class century (103) three weeks earlier against Oxford University and was still riding on that confidence – a stark contrast to his head space a year earlier on his county debut against the New Zealanders. He was caught off the bowling of wily off-spinner John Bracewell in both innings for a duck and 14.

'I just felt so out of my depth, and it made me wonder, "What am I doing here?"' Wyatt recalled. 'It showed me where I needed to get to if I wanted to make a go of county cricket. By the time I faced the West Indies things were different. I was in good form, still very innocent and I saw it as an exciting opportunity to play against this great team.'

Although Wyatt was still a county rookie, he had already faced Marshall in two County Championship matches in the 1983 season. He scored 7 and 17 in the first match at Bournemouth and wasn't out to Marshall but the friendlier pace of Tim Tremlett and Trevor Jesty as Somerset crashed to 76 all out when Marshall took 7-29.

In the second match, Wyatt managed an encouraging innings of 44 before Marshall splattered his stumps for a duck second time round. 'Before that first game at Bournemouth, which was my Championship debut, I remember telling a friend the day before, "Tomorrow is do or die!" He said, "What do you mean?" I told him, "Well, we all know about Marshall's reputation for being the fastest bowler in the world so I might not even be able to see the ball." Fortunately, I did see the ball and it calmed me down quite a bit.'

Wyatt ended the 1983 season with scores of 69 and 82 not out against a Warwickshire bowling attack comprising England trio Bob Willis, Chris Old and Norman Gifford. Somerset appointed Ian Botham as captain for 1984 and he quickly advised the promising youngster he would play an important role for the first team. That endorsement lifted his mood, which was reflected in his early-season form.

He plundered 87 against Yorkshire, when he and Peter Roebuck shared a 246-run opening partnership, while the county's overseas debutant Martin Crowe waited patiently at number three before he made just 1.

Psychologically, therefore, Wyatt was well prepared for the West Indians in terms of his game and confidence before he impressed with those top scores of 45 and 69. Marks won the toss at Taunton and elected to bat, only to see his team dismissed for just 116 in 61.3 overs. The second-highest score was extras with 23, while Jeremy Lloyds was the other Somerset batsman to register double figures with 13. Curiously, it was Harper who wreaked most damage with 5-32, including the wicket of Wyatt, bowled.

The West Indians scored 342 in reply with Gomes, Richardson, Harper and Lloyd all scoring half-centuries.

'A friend came back from a second XI game before we started our second innings,' Wyatt recalled, 'and he said, "I bet you'd like a fifty this time after going so close in the first innings." I said, "I don't mind if I get out first ball because I already feel like I've contributed something." Then first ball of the second innings, I nicked Marshall – and the wicketkeeper dropped it.

'There was no question of them not putting everything into this tour game against us, though. They were playing for their own form, Test places were up for grabs, and it was quite brutal at times. I felt like I was in a real contest every ball, and there were no free runs out there. After I hung around in the first innings, it seemed they were putting in even more effort second innings, as they didn't want me hanging around again.'

Somerset succumbed cheaply once more, bundled out this time for 125 as Marshall took 5-31 in his 19.2 overs. Wyatt was the lone survivor again and Marks was the other home batsman to reach double figures, with 17.

Wyatt eventually departed to a Marshall short ball in the second innings, caught by Richie Richardson after the ball struck him on the thumb and ballooned up to gully.

'I was sitting in our dressing room with my thumb in a bucket of ice and Clive Lloyd walked in and congratulated me on how I had played,' said Wyatt. 'That was very decent of him and nice to hear.'

There was no interaction with Somerset's very own Viv Richards that match because he wasn't playing but Wyatt's performance wasn't lost on the so-called Master Blaster. After West Indies' tour had finished, Richards returned to Taunton to visit his mates. Somerset were fielding at the time.

'He saw me and said, "What are you doing here, man, we're in the field?" I said, "Yeah, I'm 12th man." Then he gave this surprised look. He glanced out on the ground and then looked back at me and said, "Well they must have a bloody good team out then." That gave me a boost and meant a lot.'

Wyatt was fortunate to have so many high-profile, world-class influences around him in his time at Somerset between 1983 and 1989. Not only was there Richards, Botham and England spinner Marks, but also Joel Garner, Martin Crowe and Steve Waugh, who played for Somerset in 1987 and 1988.

He learned the most from Waugh, specifically the way his eternally positive attitude powered his own batting and subsequently infected team-mates with optimism. Wyatt also cherished his special times with Richards, though. They shared a partnership of 185 against Michael Holding and Derbyshire in 1985. Wyatt scored 90, while Viv hit 123.

'It was quite inspirational just to be at the other end to Viv and watch him go about his game,' Wyatt reminisced, proudly. 'He wasn't a big talker, but you got confidence from being around him and in the same team as him.

'It also brought home to me the gulf between me and Viv! I hit Mikey for a four and he walked back to his marker, picked it up and started pacing out a longer run-up about a further ten yards back. The keeper and slips were giggling, and I had to battle my way through. It was an extraordinary experience. Viv, meanwhile, just looked as comfortable as he always did.'

A century against Marshall and his Hampshire team in 1985 at Bournemouth helped Somerset to draw the game and derail Hampshire's title bid. But these were successes amongst a largely mediocre bigger picture.

Wyatt played 14 Championship matches in 1984, yet only averaged just below 18. It was a mystery that he was able to raise his game against the quality that the West Indians had, but struggle against county attacks. He did not cope well with a spell of patchy form that ultimately led to him being dropped, despite an encouraging innings of 47 against Leicestershire when Andy Roberts took seven wickets in the first innings.

'I felt good and thought I was on my way back, but they dropped me after that match, and it really affected me,' said Wyatt, alluding to the mental health problems that would later contribute to the end of his professional career. 'I was too young to understand what was happening. I took it personally and lost a lot of confidence. It was disappointing that after the West Indies tour match, I was not as consistent as I would like to have been. But still, the memory is one of the best from my career.'

Wyatt was eventually released by his beloved Somerset at 26. He wrote to other clubs for a second chance but acknowledges in hindsight he did that more because he thought he should look to extend his career, as opposed to wanting to do it. His dream had always been to play for Somerset. That was what drove him, always, to represent his local county. Once that chapter ended, he was not keen to play anywhere else.

He did not know what to do with his life then, but knew he needed employment somewhere, doing something. He had been an assistant manager of a tool hire company in Bristol but gave that up to dedicate himself to cricket. After cricket there were a few odd jobs, including being a self-employed gardener for a summer and a double-glazing salesman.

Somerset came back to him and offered him the chance to replace Dennis Breakwell and look after regional school cricket programmes and, latterly, youth coaching that included working with the second XI. He did that from 1991 to 2001.

One might think Wyatt eventually landed his ultimate position outside of playing cricket professionally, with the coaching work at Somerset. However, it was a pain for him.

'I was glad to have a job, but it wasn't at all helpful in a psychological way as it just reminded me of what I had lost,' Wyatt reflected. 'Being around the club and aspiring cricketers again was almost like a constant reminder that I once had that life before it was taken away from me. It probably took the best part of 30 years for me to come to terms with it and get over that disappointment.

'When I look back at my career, I see there were mental health issues that I needed help with, but that kind of support just wasn't there, like it is now. You had to get on with it and subsequently I struggled with confidence.

When you struggled with form in the time I played the only things that were talked about were technical. "Your head is in the wrong position, your feet aren't moving right, you're not watching the ball well enough." No one ever thought to ask, "Is your head in the right space?" Because, on too many occasions, it wasn't.

'Kapil Dev got me out in both innings when he played for Worcestershire at the end of that '84 summer, and it was like he was toying with me. He was a very skilful bowler but I was in no fit mental state to face him with where my head was at.'

The Headingley Chronicles, Third Test

Gomes: The Renaissance

*'Skipper Lloyd used to refer to Larry as the glue in our
team as he complemented the rest of the batters in our
line-up who might be more dashing. Larry was less
flamboyant but still put away the bad ball and could bat
for long periods.'* – Roger Harper

Larry Gomes was the quiet man of the West Indies team.
He didn't bludgeon the ball like Gordon Greenidge,
Viv Richards and Clive Lloyd; he wasn't as charismatic
as Desmond Haynes, Malcolm Marshall and Michael
Holding; he didn't generate headlines like many of his
team-mates. But wow, how he came of age in 1984.

Lloyd was a captain who appreciated balance in his
line-up, hence his leaning towards all-rounders like Harper
and Baptiste. Similarly, Gomes provided calm and a
steadying influence against the dashing stroke play of his
fellow batsmen.

There was little room for new faces given that
Greenidge, Haynes, Richards and Lloyd were always
going to play, and Dujon was no stranger to batting at
six either. There was, however, fierce competition for the

final batting position between Gomes, Richie Richardson and Gus Logie.

Gomes was without a half-century in 15 Test innings going into the first Test at Edgbaston. His international career was on the line and at his age then, almost 31 and nine years the senior to Richardson and seven years older than Logie, he was unlikely to have received another chance. Failure in Birmingham and it was possible that Gomes was gone for good.

'Players always know if they are not scoring runs consistently there are other players who are breathing down their necks for their place in the team,' Roger Harper commented. 'But Larry performed in a big way in this series.'

In the first Test, Gomes came good against an England attack that was short on discipline with their lines and lengths and stroked the highest score of his Test career, 143. He followed that up at Lord's with an unbeaten 92, a typically composed innings while Greenidge hammered a match-winning double century at the other end.

'Larry's innings was not unexpected as he was that kind of reliable player,' Greenidge said. 'A lot of times he steadied the ship when others around him were being more forceful, though I am not saying Larry could not play his shots because he often did, but he provided a balance.'

By the time Headingley came along Gomes was in the best form of his career. He even plundered 143 against Leicestershire between the second and third Tests. Logie also scored a century to keep the pressure on him for his place.

England responded positively from their demoralising defeat at Lord's by winning the toss, batting first and posting 270 on the back of another excellent century from Allan Lamb. It was a competitive total after being 87/4, as Lamb (100) and Ian Botham (45) added 85 for the fifth wicket.

'Harper bowled me a grubber that rolled,' Lamb recalled. 'I should have got a lot more runs there because I was going really well.'

The West Indies looked as though they would be conceding a first-innings deficit when they slumped to 206/7, with Gomes yet again propping up their batting. Holding joined him and they put on a game-changing partnership of 82 for the eighth wicket. Holding dominated the stand with his ultra-aggressive 59 from 55 balls, thumping five sixes. Gomes supported him, serenely, and finished with an unbeaten 104 as the tourists were 302 all out.

Paul Allott's outswing to the right-handers wreaked most of the damage and he finished with a Test best analysis of 6-61, on his comeback after two years out of the side. Gower was rewarded for handing Allott the new ball alongside Bob Willis, even though Botham had opened the bowling at Lord's and taken 8-103.

Joel Garner was furious with the batsmen's attitude in the first innings and felt their old weakness of overconfidence had returned to haunt them and he thought the way they made Allott look good was 'disgusting'.

'It was a typical Headingley pitch in the eighties and was the only pitch that brought the two sides closer together,' Gower recalled. 'It was always going to do a bit and Walt (Allott) was the perfect man to take the new ball with his persistent line and length, nibbling it around.'

Still, England once again surrendered a much stronger position having taken early wickets. The West Indies' tail wagged and England allowed the tourists off the hook, a common theme throughout the summer.

'We just couldn't bowl them out, we didn't have the bowlers,' Lamb said. 'That was the problem.'

Chris Broad went a step further by summing up that the bowlers they had at Headingley were the best available and that the depth amongst England's fast bowling stocks in those days was not there.

'It was telling that our fastest bowler was someone who was coming to the end of his career (Willis),' Broad suggested. 'We had Fozzy, Norman Cowans, Pring, bowlers who were not going to knock the top off their batting order in batsman-friendly conditions, so it was always going to be difficult.

'If you have someone with that extra pace or x-factor it can make a difference when conditions are flat. David "Teddy" Thomas from Surrey, being left arm, might have made a difference, who knows. We had what we had.'

Pat Pocock, meantime, also suggested that his Surrey team-mate Thomas might have been a shrewd option that England should have looked at that summer, because of his extra pace.

'We would stand back about 24 yards behind the stumps to Sylvester Clarke, who was widely feared on the county circuit,' Pocock said. 'But what was interesting was that we would stand back the same distance for "Teddy" Thomas. He was a lively, quick bowler. Thomas and Clarke together were a real handful for county batsmen. Teddy was probably the quickest English bowler around then but because he wasn't picked for a Test, he was generally unappreciated.'

England's batsmen were less competitive in the second innings as Marshall's exhibition of quality fast bowling destroyed them. Marshall, bowling with a broken thumb in a plaster cast, claimed his Test best figures of 7-53 and it was 3-0 after a comfortable chase of just 128 runs – and no surprises that Gomes was there at the end. England had not lost the first three Tests of a home series since 1921 against Australia.

Typical of yet another vital but understated Gomes contribution, he was overshadowed by Marshall's bowling performance, as he had been by Richards and Garner at Edgbaston and by Greenidge at Lord's. Gomes often flew beneath the radar, but his team-mates certainly appreciated the role he played in that game and the series generally.

'Skipper Lloyd used to refer to Larry as the glue in our team as he complemented the rest of the batters in our line-up who might be more dashing,' Harper commented. 'Larry was less flamboyant but still put away the bad ball and could bat for long periods. He was also a very nice guy who got along with almost everyone. He wouldn't be jumping out in front to attract all the attention. He just went about his business in a quiet manner.'

Garner sympathised with the challenge that the England bowlers had in bowling at Gomes that summer, as he gave nothing away and always provided the perfect balance to their batting.

'Gomes is a tiresome batsman to bowl at,' Garner said at the time. 'He seldom appears to be making runs because he rarely strikes the ball ferociously. Instead, he approaches his highest scores in crab-like fashion, cautiously and rather sideways. He walks to the wicket and appears to be doing nothing for a while until you look at the scoreboard and he has 40-something. The next moment he's raising his bat for a century that he reached with more stealth than a pickpocket.'

This tour was something of a renaissance for the left-handed Trinidadian as he had extensive experience of English conditions, yet he had rarely mastered them prior to this tour.

Gomes first toured England in 1970 with West Indies Young Cricketers, then played for Middlesex second XI in 1972 and the Middlesex main team from 1973 through to 1975 along with the likes of Mike Brearley, Fred Titmus, Phil Edmonds and J.T. Murray. Gomes' fifth first-class match was in the County Championship against Clive Lloyd and Lancashire at Old Trafford in 1973.

He toured England with the West Indies in 1976, making his Test debut there, but managed only scores of 0, 11 and 0.

He missed the 1980 England tour and by the early eighties was still in and out of the side, as he competed with the likes of Alvin Kallicharran, Faoud Bacchus and Everton Mattis for the final batting position, a role he still found himself in until he nailed down the number three spot in 1984. By then, he was well appreciated by players from both teams.

Jeff Dujon: 'He played his role perfectly, helping to extend an innings and made sure nothing happened at one end. The attacking players could get on with it from the other end. This was an important summer for him with the younger Richardson waiting in the wings, and Logie too to a lesser extent. Richie came into his own later, but at this point Larry was a very good steadying influence at the top of the innings.

Allan Lamb: 'Gomes was a good player, and he had a great summer. He wasn't a forceful player, was more of a dabber and just slowly picked up his runs.'

Derek Pringle: 'It felt like you had to bowl even wider of off stump than to Viv Richards because Gomes was a master at clipping everything down to fine leg to get off strike. He didn't try to intimidate you like Viv, Clive and Gordon, but if you bowled him a bad ball he would put it away.'

David Gower: 'The Headingley pitch offered something to both teams and it says a lot about the West Indies, and especially Larry, that they had the ability to get themselves out of trouble.

'His method was pretty simple. He basically got himself in good positions, watched the ball well, nudged it away a lot, dropped the bat on it often, left it well, but still put the bad ball away. He got into form and stayed in form.

'The flamboyant guys like Greenidge, Haynes, Richards and Lloyd, they were the icons of the batting line-up who could smash it everywhere with more than enough strokes between them. Larry was their foundation. If they had a blistering start, it wasn't an issue. If they lost an early wicket, Larry came in, nudged it around for five hours and the job was done.'

HEADINGLEY SCORECARD:

England

	First Innings		Second Innings	
G. Fowler	lbw b Garner	10	c & b Marshall	50
B.C. Broad	c Lloyd b Harper	32	c Baptiste b Marshall	2
V.P. Terry	c Harper b Holding	8	lbw b Garner	1
D.I. Gower	lbw b Garner	2	c Dujon b Harper	43
A.J. Lamb	b Harper	100	lbw b Marshall	3
I.T. Botham	c Dujon b Baptiste	45	c Dujon b Garner	14
P.R. Downton	c Lloyd b Harper	17	c Dujon b Marshall	27
D.R. Pringle	c Haynes b Harper	19	(9) lbw b Marshall	2
P.J.W. Allott	b Holding	3	(10) lbw b Marshall	4
N.G.B. Cook	b Holding	1	(8) c Lloyd b Marshall	0
R.G.D. Willis	not out	4	not out	5
97.2 overs, extras 29		270	65 overs, 8 extras	159

Fall of wickets 1st innings: 1-13 (Fowler); 2-43 (Terry); 3-53 (Gower); 4-87 (Broad); 5-172 (Botham); 6-236 (Downton); 7-237 (Lamb); 8-244 (Allott); 9-254 (Cook); 10-270 (Pringle).

Bowling: Garner 30-11-73-2; Marshall 6-4-6-0; Holding 29.2-8-70-4; Baptiste 13-1-45-1; Harper 19-6-47-3

Fall of wickets 2nd Innings: 1-10 (Broad); 2-13 (Terry); 3-104 (Gower); 4-106 (Fowler); 5-107 (Lamb); 6-135 (Botham); 7-138 (Cook); 8-140 (Pringle); 9-146 (Allott); 10-159 (Downton)

Bowling: Garner 16-7-37-2; Marshall 26-9-53-7; Holding 7-1-31-0; Harper 16-8-30-1

West Indies

	First Innings		Second Innings	
C.G. Greenidge	c Botham b Willis	10	c Terry b Cook	49
D.L. Haynes	b Allott	18	c Fowler b Cook	43
H.A. Gomes	not out	104	not out	2

I.V.A. Richards	c Pringle b Allott	15	not out	22
C.H. Lloyd	c Gower b Cook	48		
P.J. Dujon	lbw b Allott	26		
E.A.E. Baptiste	c Broad b Allott	0		
R.A. Harper	c Downton b Allott	0		
M.A. Holding	c Allott b Willis	59		
J. Garner	run out	0		
M.D. Marshall	c Botham b Allott	4		
73.5 overs, 18 extras		302	32.3 overs, 2 wkts, 15 ex.	131

Fall of wickets 1st Innings: 1-16 (Greenidge); 2-43 (Haynes); 3-78 (Richards); 4-148 (Lloyd); 5-201 (Dujon); 6-206 (Baptiste); 7-206 (Harper); 8-288 (Holding); 9-290 (Garner); 10-302 (Marshall)

Bowling: Willis 18-1-123-2; Allott 26.5-7-61-6; Botham 7-0-45-0; Pringle 13-3-26-0; Cook 9-1-29-1

Fall of wickets 2nd Innings: 1-106 (Haynes); 2-108 (Greenidge)

Bowling: Willis 8-1-40-0; Allott 7-2-24-0; Pringle 8.3-2-25-0; Cook 9-2-27-2

Toss: England, elected to bat first

Player of the match: Larry Gomes

West Indies won by 8 wickets

Marshall – The One-Armed Genius

'The longer (Malcolm) played the better he became. He was able to move the ball around and bowl a bouncer that sat you on your backside whenever he wanted to.' –
Chris Broad

Clive Lloyd sat in the Headingley dressing room with his key fast-bowling spearhead Malcolm Marshall, who was nursing a double fracture of his left thumb sustained while fielding at gully in England's first innings. The West Indies were already 2-0 up in the series, but this third Test hung in the balance at the halfway stage.

Lloyd looked at Marshall and said, 'Do you want to bowl?' Marshall said, 'Well, I have this broken thumb, skip?' To which Lloyd replied: 'I know but I'm asking *do you want to bowl?*'

There was a brief silence, but once Marshall realised his captain was banking on him to go to war for him and his team-mates, and once Lloyd had received the reaction he had hoped for from Marshall, it was clear that England's batsmen were going to be disappointed if they had expected 'Maco' to take the easy way out and sit and watch proceedings from the players' balcony.

'Malcolm was the best fast bowler I ever captained because he was so intelligent,' Lloyd said. 'He had pace but so much more with it.

'Once I knew he was up for having a bowl, I suggested we find him some tape to wrap over his white plaster that was covering his damaged hand. I didn't want England to have any excuses to stop Malcolm from bowling.'

It wasn't Marshall's first act of bravery for his team, as he had already batted one-handed and even managed to score a boundary off Paul Allott. The reason he had gone into bat with the injury was to enable Larry Gomes to reach three figures.

Gomes made 104 not out in the event before Marshall gave Allott his sixth wicket, caught by Botham at second slip.

Thereafter, it was all about Marshall the bowler and his Test best 7-53 in 26 overs that helped bowl England out for 159, before the tourists were able to cruise to an eight-wicket victory. The broken bone, which restricted him to just six overs in England's first innings, worked against England as Marshall did not try to bowl as quickly as normal, but instead used the conditions and swung the ball.

Marshall's Hampshire colleague Paul Terry made his Test debut in the match and struggled to make an impact, scoring just 8 and 1. He was full of admiration for their attack and believes he was not quite ready then for such a challenge in hindsight.

'Maco was probably the best bowler in the world then and Joel Garner and Michael Holding weren't far behind,' Terry said. 'It was a pretty awesome attack and mentally I wasn't ready for that challenge then. I probably needed more time in county cricket to establish myself.

'That's how I felt after my debut, but you never give up the opportunity to play for your country. Ideally, I would have been given another chance later in my career when I was better prepared, but it never came.'

This Test match was a watershed moment in Marshall's development as a match-winning bowler as he learned that speed was merely one of his many weapons and he didn't always have to bowl flat out to compete with his fellow fast bowlers.

He realised he had the skills to dismiss batsmen without having to rely purely on pace. Those skills improved as he got older.

Chris Broad was the first to depart to Marshall for 2, and it wasn't swing that did for him but bounce that surprised him off a good length as he could only lob the ball up to Eldine Baptiste at backward square leg.

'I am often asked the best fast bowler I faced and I played with one at Notts, Richard Hadlee, who was outstanding, especially against right-handers,' Broad said. 'But with Marshall the longer he played the better he became. He was able to move the ball around and bowl a bouncer that sat you on your backside whenever he wanted to. He was a very clever bowler.'

England at one stage looked as though they would make the West Indies fight for their victory as Graeme Fowler and David Gower added 91 for the third wicket. But once Roger Harper removed Gower, it was 'The Marshall Show'. He claimed six of the last seven wickets as England collapsed from 104/2 to 159 all out.

'Maco was special and I always say one of the reasons I went to Hampshire was to be on the same side as him,' Gower said with a grin. 'Malcolm was mighty clever and even though these pitches weren't like Barbados where the bounce was climbing into your chest, he still had the ability to pitch it up and swing it, at good pace.'

Fowler was deceived by a change of pace to give a return catch to Marshall for 50, Allan Lamb was trapped in front to a ball that nipped back brutishly, and suddenly it was 107/5. That's how games could change in an instant against this attack, or notably against Marshall.

Once Joel Garner removed Ian Botham, Marshall accounted for the tail for just 14 further runs. It was all over pretty much. The final wicket of Paul Downton, who fought bravely for an hour and a half for his 27 runs, gave Marshall his 700th first-class wicket and, at that point, his best analysis in Test matches.

'Lloydy would tell me to warm up, but Malcolm kept asking for "one more over",' Eldine Baptiste remembered. 'He didn't want to give that ball up. In the end I didn't get a bowl. He was awesome, it was an incredible spell.'

Downton added: 'I tried to hang in there, but Marshall just blew us away and we didn't really compete in the second innings.'

When this author canvassed 100 cricket greats to select their World XI for the book *In A League of Their Own*, Marshall made it into the final 'Ultimate XI' from the weight of votes. In fact, Marshall selected his own side but was too modest to pick himself!

When such a topic is debated it is inevitable the likes of Wasim Akram, Glenn McGrath, Michael Holding, Dennis Lillee, Richard Hadlee, Fred Trueman and others such as Dale Steyn and James Anderson from the modern era all come into contention. But more often than not, Marshall would be favoured by the majority, from those who saw him anyway.

Marshall retired from Test cricket in 1991, but his record of 376 wickets in 81 matches at an average of 20.94 has stood the test of time, to phrase it modestly.

There was a lot more to Marshall's magic than simply the performer we saw on the day on the big stage. So much thought and practice went into his skill set, and it ultimately led to him becoming the greatest fast bowler certainly of his day, maybe ever.

'Me and Malcolm were roommates, and we would talk about cricket all the time,' Baptiste revealed. 'He was young then, but I still learnt a lot from him. Maybe the thing I remember most was how he judged himself and always wanted to improve.

'Later that year (1984), in Australia, I was 12th man and he asked me to watch him closely. He said, "When I come off, I want you to tell me what I'm doing wrong or what I can do better." I said, "Nah Maco, I can't do that, you're my senior." But he insisted, so when he came off, I would occasionally say things like, "Maco, you're bowling too short, you need to pitch it up a bit more because you're too good to be going at four runs an over." He was always critiquing himself. And he had an encyclopaedic knowledge of batsmen's strengths and weaknesses. He was a phenomenal bowler and the head of our pack.

'And that wasn't by coincidence. He worked so hard at his game. On that Australia tour, he was struggling to bring the ball back into the right-hander. But he practised so hard on that tour that it was amazing how quickly he mastered that skill.

'He bowled such a dangerous length that batsmen would hang back but then he would skid one through and do them for pace when they should have been forward. He bowled so intelligently.'

That latter trickery that Baptiste alluded to was one of Marshall's greatest strengths. He was a thinking man's fast bowler. There is an old-fashioned, outdated cliché that fast bowlers are not blessed with the brains that other types of cricketers might have. Whoever came up with that saying certainly would not have had Malcolm Denzil Marshall in mind.

Gordon Greenidge was a team-mate of Marshall not only with the West Indies but also at Hampshire and Barbados. He knew the fast bowler better than anyone.

'Malcolm was a great conman with the ball, whereby he would sucker the batsman in and then lay him out flat,' said Greenidge.

'I'm sure he was a good influence on the younger bowlers that we had coming through over the years like Courtney Walsh, Curtly Ambrose and Patrick Patterson. Because Malcolm was able to do the things he was teaching and when he said something, people listened. He was a genius with a cricket ball.'

The Old Trafford Chronicles, Fourth Test

Lamb's (West) Indian Summer

'My philosophy was you had to look to score runs. If you let them bowl six balls out of six to you every over, you were knackered because they would get you out soon enough.' – Allan Lamb

This series would have been a tad weird for Allan Lamb, or certainly bittersweet.

It was, after all, the best summer of his career – three centuries against the world-leading West Indies and then a fourth against Sri Lanka. But it just happened to coincide with one of England's worst ever beatings. Therefore, it was not as though he was ever going to sit in the dressing room at The Oval after the fifth Test and feel especially smug with himself when his team had just suffered a 5-0 thrashing.

'Yes, I did okay, but when I look back, I can't see past the 5-0,' Lamb reflected. 'Personal success doesn't mean as much when compared to team success. Winning the Ashes home and away felt much better. The only time my success against the West Indies really felt good was when we beat them in Jamaica (in 1990), and I got a hundred there. That means so much more when I look back.'

Lamb repaid the faith of the selectors in '84 after he had endured miserable tours to New Zealand and Pakistan earlier in the year. He could point to the runs he had scored for England previously, though, that marked him as someone to persevere with, such as his encouraging first overseas tour for England in Australia in 1982/83 where he made 72, 82 and 83.

'I played well there and should have capitalised and scored a couple of hundreds,' Lamb said. 'It was a tough tour, but because of my upbringing in South Africa where attitudes were similar, I knew what it was all about and slotted in okay.'

The Old Trafford Test saw Lamb register his third century in as many matches. It was a significant reversal of fortunes given he started the series in something of a form rut. Whereas his team-mates struggled all series to enjoy any superiority over the West Indies bowlers – only Graeme Fowler also reached three figures – Lamb relished the battle against their pace attack, which he felt needed to be attacked as opposed to a more cautious approach.

Lamb considered his upbringing in South Africa as a key in his technique that served him so well in the summer of 1984, after batting on fast and bouncy pitches against quality pace bowlers such as Clive Rice, Vince van der Bijl, Mike Procter and Garth Le Roux.

'I tried to keep things very simple and my philosophy was you had to look to score runs,' said Lamb. 'If you let them bowl six balls out of six to you every over, you were knackered because they would get you out soon enough.

'It's also important to rotate the strike. You can't hit every ball, but make sure you are looking for your runs and when they do bowl something you can hit, make sure you chuck your bat at it. Yes, it's important to occupy the crease but you have to score runs.'

Many of the players from both sides admired the way Lamb went about his business in this series – his England team-mates appreciated his runs and the West Indies admired and respected his courage and aggression to fight fire with fire.

David Gower: 'Allan was one of the few who fully embraced the immense challenge ahead of us and did reasonably well. The way he played against that West Indies team that year and against them in that era generally said a lot about his calibre as a player, and about his character, guts and determination. It was a huge disappointment, and to him personally, that he couldn't translate that form to the Ashes and against other teams (he scored one century in 20 Ashes Tests). If you could score runs against the West Indies in the eighties, that really took some doing so at least he can be proud of that.'

Eldine Baptiste: 'His mentality was good, he looked to score, he wasn't looking to survive. He had the right approach as those who tried to hang around would end up getting out. Lamby scored a lot of runs to third man as Lloydy and the other bowlers didn't like a third man, but I did. Lamby liked to cut and drive, so good luck to him for executing his shots. He was positive and not apprehensive like the other England batsmen. But when the ball bounced, he would get leg side of the ball and cut, so that's why I wanted a third man. I always said the ball to get Lamby was the one that nipped back because he was looser than the others and he created that gap (between bat and pad).'

Chris Broad: 'If you look at a few of the South African players we've had in the team down the years they are generally very good against pace because they are brought up on faster bowling whereas we are probably more accustomed to slower bowling that does a bit. Robin Smith and Chris Smith were other examples. They coped very well against pace.'

Roger Harper: 'He gave us a lot of trouble. He was very competitive and always looked to score and handled the short ball very well.'

Jeff Dujon: 'From the first time I played against him he had this uncanny knack of getting runs against us. He was a great player, and a good guy. The Old Trafford pitch itself was seaming about a bit and we bowled well. The funny thing about Lamby was that technically I didn't think he was that tight, but he had a very good eye and was a great timer of the ball. If you gave him any room outside off stump he was on it and I don't recall him nicking too many out there. He scored quite freely. He was a bit of an enigma because he wasn't so technical but was a great attacker and would take the fight to you.'

Paul Terry: 'He played superbly, was much more experienced than me and had a great method against the short ball. It was exceptional for him to get those runs on wickets that were up and down against their incredible bowling attack. He was predominantly a back foot player, and it served him well in this series and made him stand out amongst the English players.'

Clive Lloyd: 'Most teams had that one person who gave us problems, like Jimmy (Amarnath) from India, AB (Border) from Australia. Lamby took us on a bit more than the others, so deserved his runs.'

Allan Lamb *(Asked what he thought about the challenge of Marshall, who seemed to trouble him more than other bowlers Lamb said):* 'People have brought it up over the years as Maco got me out 13 times in my career (7 lbw), but I also got runs against him. He was a great bowler as he swung the ball both ways, he had a real quick bouncer and was clever, he knew exactly where to put the ball and what to do with it.

'Look, he was the best fast bowler I ever faced, but it wasn't like I never scored runs against him. It didn't always help me, but I could read him from the hand. I knew if his wrist position stayed up it would be a fuller length but once he cocked that wrist it was going to be short. I naturally just picked that up.'

Clive Lloyd won the toss and batted on a ground he knew well. He may soon have regretted the decision when his team crashed to 70/4 as his Lancashire team-mate Paul Allott followed on from his success at Headingley to remove three of the top four cheaply.

It wasn't the first occasion in the series where England considered themselves right in the game, only to see it slip away from them because they lacked the bowling firepower to finish off what they had started. West Indies still found a way to reach 500.

West Indies supporters celebrate after the fifth Test at The Oval, where their team completed what some fans nicknamed a 'Black Wash'.

The victorious West Indies touring squad of 1984. Winston Davis was added to the squad from the fourth Test.

Botham could rarely resist the hook shot and West Indies' bowlers saw it as an obvious way to dismiss him. At Edgbaston, umpire Dickie Bird deemed Malcolm Marshall had bowled too many short balls at Botham and warned him for intimidatory tactics.

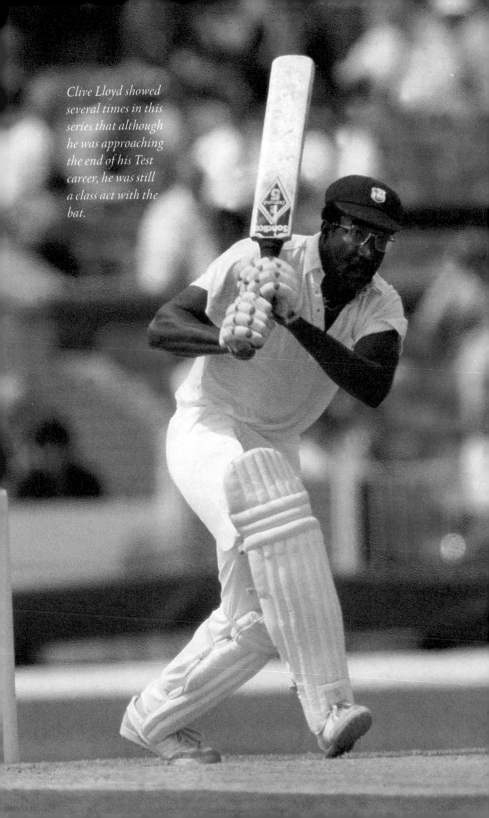

Clive Lloyd showed several times in this series that although he was approaching the end of his Test career, he was still a class act with the bat.

Joel Garner enjoyed a new lease of life when taking the new ball in England in '84, taking nine wickets in the first Test in Birmingham.

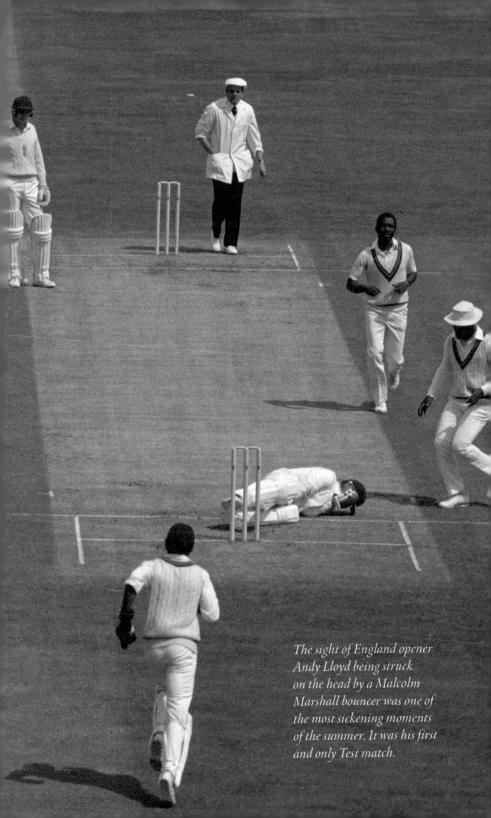

The sight of England opener Andy Lloyd being struck on the head by a Malcolm Marshall bouncer was one of the most sickening moments of the summer. It was his first and only Test match.

Gordon Greenidge was in imperious form during the series, notching double centuries at both Lord's and Old Trafford. Here, he drives aggressively down the ground as Paul Downton looks on from behind the stumps.

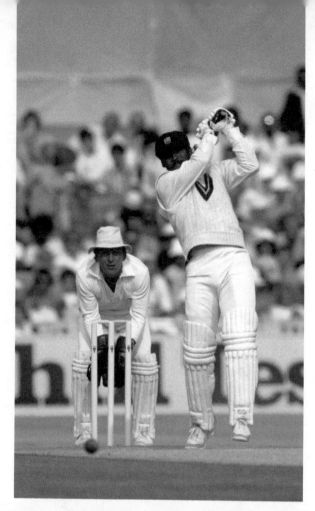

The West Indies slip fielders rarely made an error and brilliantly supported their pace battery (from the left, Joel Garner, Gordon Greenidge, Roger Harper, Viv Richards and Clive Lloyd, at Headingley).

Malcolm Marshall batted with a broken wrist to allow Larry Gomes to reach his century in the third Test.

Malcolm Marshall, bowling with a broken wrist, still managed a career best 7-53 at Leeds.

The recall of Surrey off-spinner Pat Pocock for the fourth and fifth Tests was something of a shock after he had been out of the side since 1976. He subsequently earned himself a place on the winter tour to India.

Viv Richards on the attack in his innings of 189 not out in the first one-day international at Old Trafford. That effort broke English hearts when they had expected to win the match. How much did this innings and the result subsequently influence the Test series? Probably quite a lot.

'Throughout the whole of that series we didn't have the bowlers to finish them off and that was a big problem,' Lamb said. 'Beefy was on his own, we really struggled. Yes, we should have scored more runs than we did also, though quite often we created opportunities with the ball but just allowed them to get away from us plenty of times.'

Gordon Greenidge proved himself a nuisance again, plundering his second double century in three Tests for 223, and he was joined by Jeffrey Dujon, who had endured a poor series to this point. Dujon made 101 and helped put on a match-defining partnership of 197 for the fifth wicket.

Dujon, unlike most of his fellow tourists, hadn't played first-team county cricket, but he still had plenty of experience playing in the UK. He had seven games for Glamorgan's second XI and Glamorgan under-25s in 1977. This was after he spent a summer in Wales with his former school coach Ron Jones, the ex-BBC commentator, to sample English conditions.

He had also scored 62 at Lord's in 1974 for West Indies Young Cricketers against England. By the time he returned in 1983 for the World Cup he had a fair idea of the conditions. He said batting with Greenidge for a length of time helped him to feel his way into his innings and, subsequently, the series.

'I remember being at the non-striker's end and watching Gordon Greenidge just hammering the ball,' Dujon recalled. 'That took a lot of pressure off me, and it was a good track too. I felt that I hadn't done enough in the series to that point, so I thought this was a chance to get my head down and try to get a score.

'The way Gordon played helped as I didn't have to be in a rush. Gordon's innings was something else, he was in total command. He really was on top of his game, dominating.'

Greenidge averaged 100.60 in his four Tests at Old Trafford, figures that bizarrely include three centuries and a duck in 1980 when dismissed by Graham Dilley. He stopped short of admitting that 1984 was his best form despite a second double century in the series.

'I wouldn't say it was my peak as I didn't play too bad in 1976 either with those consecutive hundreds in Manchester,' Greenidge commented. He was a renowned power hitter but maybe not credited enough for the application he also showed at times, like in 1984 when steering his team from jeopardy at 70/4.

'I always tried to get the best out of myself no matter how difficult the challenge,' he added. 'That's how you learn about the game and about yourself, too. I didn't always look fashionable or play the textbook style but that was the way I preferred to play and handle matters. That was just me. There is individualism everywhere you look, everyone has their own traits. I never wanted to be a batsman that was good to look at, I wanted to be a batsman who was successful.'

England wicketkeeper Paul Downton had the pleasure, though he would not have regarded the experience as such at the time, of watching every one of Greenidge's runs that summer. He believed him to be at the top of his game then.

'He was one of the most aggressive batsmen in the world, especially severe to anything short,' Downton said.

'It seemed to be his time. We contained him up to a point, but it was difficult to keep him quiet.

'It was 70/4 at lunch and after the interval they put their foot down and went after us. We couldn't exert any control and lost a bit of discipline, though the spinners bowled okay. Allowing them to get away from us at 70/4 was the game-changing moment.'

Dujon was a 'flowery stroke maker', according to Gower, who had plenty lot of shots and liked to play them. 'Dujon batted at seven most of the time for the West Indies but he would have been a number four or five for any other team,' Paul Terry insisted. 'He got them out of trouble quite often and was so good to watch.'

Even when Dujon's four-hour innings was ended by Ian Botham, nightwatchman Winston Davis added a painful 170 runs with Greenidge as he crashed the English attack all around Old Trafford. He made 77 in three hours.

Davis was only called up from his spell at Glamorgan after Milton Small was sent home, with a knee injury. Davis was wiry, strong, able to bowl for long spells and could shape the ball away and nip it back. He also possessed a nasty bouncer. He learned the night before the Test that he would be playing as replacement for Marshall, who'd suffered a double fracture of his thumb at Headingley. It upset Courtney Walsh initially as he was already in the original squad, but those feelings of hurt were soon remedied by the skipper.

'I was a little disappointed not to play ahead of Winston,' Walsh said. 'But Clive came and spoke to me and said, "Youngster, we're bringing in Winston from

Glamorgan. Just stay patient and your time will come." He didn't have to do that. I respected him for it and appreciated that Winston was doing well at the time so if it was best for the team, I was okay with it. And my chance did come on the following tour, to Australia.'

It was during Davis's partnership with Greenidge that Gower would have known things were not destined to go his way, in this match or the series. Davis, though, felt England had only themselves to blame.

'Every fast bowler likes to think he can bat,' Davis reflected with a glint in his eye. 'We like to hit the ball. My job initially was to protect Gordon, so getting runs was a bonus.

'When I batted, I always hung back, and hardly ever pushed forward. The English bowlers made a mistake in trying to bounce me out, but it suited my game. I was happy to keep playing the pull and hook shots. Bowlers like Paul Allott and Norman Cowans were never going to bother me bowling short at their pace, but if they had pitched the ball up more then I am sure they would have taken my wicket. I wasn't intending on poking around.'

The most successful bowler for England was veteran off-spinner Pat Pocock, recalled after an eight-year absence. He took 4-121 from 45.3 overs of toil and showed there was spin for the slow bowlers. Dujon felt England got their selection wrong by opting for two spinners, like at Edgbaston.

'England's problem was their batsmen so they should have replaced one of the spinners with an extra batsman,' Dujon said. 'The pitch was a bit up and down, but had they played with an extra batsman they would have got more runs. Their tail looked a bit on the long side at times, especially when Ian Botham wasn't able to contribute at six.'

England drafted Cowans in for his first Test of the summer to bowl seam alongside Botham and Allott. Richard Ellison said he had been selected initially but had to settle for being 12th man after feeling unwell on the morning of the match. Ellison made his debut in the next Test instead.

Middlesex man Cowans went wicketless and was soon dropped again for the fifth match, where Ellison and Jonathan Agnew came in. It was a sequence that Cowans had sadly become accustomed to. New Zealand legend Richard Hadlee was an admirer of Cowans and he felt captains Bob Willis and then Gower handled him badly. From his county experiences with Notts, he felt Cowans was one of few bowlers in England with pace and who should have been treated better, after his six wickets at the MCG. Instead, he felt they questioned minor technical frailties that crushed his confidence.

Mike Gatting played with and captained Cowans for many years at Middlesex and he appreciated the skills he brought to any team he played in. The two of them, fortunately for Cowans, were reunited on the 1984/85 tour to India where Cowans bowled selflessly on pitches that favoured the spinners. Gower said Cowans was 'bloody useful' in India and bowled with pace and swung the ball at times.

'Norman was a fantastic bowler you could rely on,' Gatting said, 'and he very rarely bowled a bad spell or got whacked. He had a good action with a nice upright seam, would get the ball to swing around and nip about and at good pace. He had some serious pace when he first came on the scene as a youngster. With the people that were around then, yes, he might well have been underused.

'It was always a case of what the selectors were looking for at a given time. Possibly Norman suffered from the fact there were so many quality seamers around at Middlesex then with Wayne (Daniel), Neil Williams, Simon Hughes, Gussy (Angus Fraser) came through, and we also had Vintcent van der Bijl for one season at Lord's, so there was plenty of competition for Norman at Middlesex, as well as England. That's one reason why his quality may have been missed more than it should have been.'

The Jamaica-born Cowans said he was just pleased to be given an opportunity at Old Trafford, but it was short-lived and not especially successful against an inspired Greenidge.

'There was no margin for error,' Cowans reflected. 'Usually on English wickets the ball did a bit, but Gordon had been playing in English conditions for a decade by 1984 so he was very accustomed to our environment. And the pitches were quite flat and slow that summer, so it was all weighted in his favour. But he was at the top of his game. I just tried to contain him in that match, as the ball and pitch were doing nothing for the bowlers.'

It was ironic that although England spent the whole summer fearing the relentless impact of West Indies' four-pronged pace attack, it was their 6ft 5in Guyanese off-spinner Roger Harper who dealt the last rites here in Manchester, with a deadly spell of 6-57.

It was equally ironic that England picked two spinners in the match and neither Pocock nor Cook were able to trouble the West Indians enough to push England towards victory. Harper, though, became the first West Indies spin bowler since Lance Gibbs 22 years earlier to take six wickets in an innings against England.

Harper was wicketless in the first innings but benefitted from captain Lloyd's experience at the ground.

'It was known in those days as a ground that encouraged the spinners and it certainly worked out that way for me,' Harper said. 'The captain had played many years on the ground for Lancashire and he saw that Pocock had been getting a lot of turn from the other end to the one I had been bowling from so he switched me. It worked out well – and only one of my six wickets was a left-hander.'

The England batsmen were won over by Harper's match-winning spell.

Chris Broad: 'He wasn't a big turner of the ball, though I wasn't as adept at playing the slower bowlers as I was the faster bowlers.'

David Gower: 'Take nothing away from Roger, if you get a six-for at Test level you've earned it. And he earned it.'

Paul Downton: 'From my own side, I focused so hard against the fast bowlers that sometimes, when Harper came on, subconsciously I thought, "This is my opportunity to score some runs." So he may have benefitted in that way, though he bowled well in fairness to him on a pitch that offered him some assistance.'

OLD TRAFFORD SCORECARD

West Indies

First Innings

C.G. Greenidge	c Downton b Pocock	223
D.L. Haynes	c Cowans b Botham	2
H.A. Gomes	c Botham b Allott	30
I.V.A. Richards	c Cook b Allott	1
C.H. Lloyd	c Downton b Allott	1
P.J. Dujon	c Downton b Botham	101
W.W. Davis	b Pocock	77
E.A.E. Baptiste	b Pocock	6
R.A. Harper	not out	39
M.A. Holding	b Cook	0
J. Garner	c Terry b Pocock	7
160.3 overs, 13 extras		500

Fall of wickets: 1-11 (Haynes); 2-60 (Gomes); 3-62 (Richards); 4-70 (Lloyd); 5-267 (Dujon); 6-437 (Davis); 7-443 (Baptiste); 8-470 (Greenidge); 9-471 (Holding); 10-500 (Garner)

Bowling: Botham 29-5-100-2; Cowans 19-2-76-0; Allott 28-9-76-3; Cook 39-6-114-1; Pocock 45.3-14-121-4

England

	First Innings		*Second Innings (following on)*	
G. Fowler	b Baptiste	38	b Holding	0
B.C. Broad	c Harper B Davis	42	lbw b Harper	21
V.P. Terry	b Garner	7	absent hurt	
D.I. Gower	c Dujon b Baptiste	4	not out	57
A.J. Lamb	not out	100	b Harper	9
I.T. Botham	c Garner b Baptiste	6	c Haynes b Harper	1
P.R. Downton	c Harper b Garner	0	(3) b Harper	24
P.J.W. Allott	c Gomes b Davis	26	(7) b Garner	14
N.G.B. Cook	b Holding	13	(8) c Dujon b Garner	0
P.I. Pocock	b Garner	0	(9) c Garner b Harper	0
N.G. Cowans	b Garner	0	(10) b Harper	14
105.2 overs, 44 extras		280	66.4 overs, 16 extras,	
			9 wkts,	156

Fall of wickets 1st Innings: 1-90 (Fowler); 1-105 (Terry, ret. hurt); 2-112 (Broad); 3-117 (Gower); 4-138 (Botham); 5-147 (Downton); 6-228 (Allott); 7-257 (Cook); 8-278 (Pocock); 9-278 (Cowans); 10-280 (Terry)

Bowling: Garner 22.2-7-51-4; Davis 20-2-71-2; Harper 23-10-33-0; Holding 21-2-50-1; Baptiste 19-8-31-3

Fall of wickets 2nd Innings: 1-0 (Fowler); 2-39 (Broad); 3-77 (Downton); 4-99 (Lamb); 5-101 (Botham); 6-125 (Allott); 7-127 (Cook); 8-128 (Pocock); 9-156 (Cowans)

Bowling: Garner 12-4-25-2; Davis 3-1-6-0; Harper 28.4-12-57-6; Holding 11-2-21-1; Baptiste 11-5-29-0; Richards 1-0-2-0

Toss: West Indies, elected to bat first

Player of the match: Gordon Greenidge

West Indies won by an innings and 64 runs

The Unheralded Ones

'I came into a team where the fast bowlers were dominating games over a long period already, so, there was no need for me to be crying in the corner, it was more about how I could contribute to make the team better.' – Roger Harper

Whenever West Indies' greatest team is debated the 1984 side features prominently, yet there is often a rider that highlights how another version might have been stronger because ... 'Andy Roberts was quicker (or better) than Eldine Baptiste' or 'Lance Gibbs was a more skilful spinner than Roger Harper' or 'Colin Croft and Andy Roberts were superior to Winston Davis'.

Put simply, Harper, Baptiste and Davis will not be remembered in history as all-time greats individually, but the results that were achieved in 1984 and around that time were based upon vital contributions throughout the team and those three all played key roles at various stages to ensure a 5-0 series victory. An effective 'team' will generally achieve more than individuals and the captain Clive Lloyd knew that better than anyone and therefore has no hesitation in naming the 1984 side as West Indies' best. 'That team in 1984 was the best all-round team we ever had,' Lloyd said.

Eldine Baptiste played in ten Test matches and won them all – maybe there was a hint of coincidence given West Indies' dominance in that period, but he must have been doing something right to help towards that outcome. He was an all-rounder capable of chipping in with important runs, bowling long spells while keeping the run rate to a minimum, and his fielding could be spectacular as evidenced with the run-out of Geoff Miller in the Lord's Test.

Baptiste always dreamt of playing cricket for a living and grew up listening to *Test Match Special* on BBC radio. Young Eldine would listen intently and became aware of so many celebrated names such as Derek Underwood and Alan Knott – it was then a dream come true that he was able to share a dressing room with both when he eventually played for Kent, from 1980, after impressing on an Antiguan Schools tour of England in 1979.

County cricket was an invaluable learning ground for Baptiste's early development with bat and ball and was the reason why he was so well equipped to bowl tight spells against England in 1984. He later perfected his outswinger after advice from Australia's Terry Alderman at Kent.

'It was extremely useful to learn about English conditions in my early days,' Baptiste acknowledged. 'For instance, if a ball is pitched on leg stump in England when it's swinging, it can still hit off stump. But in Antigua, anything pitched on leg stump would be clipped away for four. That also meant, as a batter, you had to play the ball later. It can be a different pitch every day in England: sometimes green with seam, other times it might swing, or not. So, by the time I played for the West Indies in England in '84 I knew the conditions very well as I had played at all of the grounds.'

Baptiste is the one seamer in the 1984 attack who would routinely be mentioned last, if at all, when anecdotes are recalled from that summer. The compliments, generally, all centred around Malcolm Marshall, Joel Garner and Michael Holding, though Baptiste still played his part. England's left-handed opener Graeme Fowler admitted that he found Baptiste difficult to face because 'he wasn't as quick, but he leaned back and angled the ball across me at an acute angle and was awkward'. It's interesting that while Baptiste's eight wickets in the five Tests at 33.12 do not make spectacular reading, the batsmen he dismissed reveals more about his effectiveness. He accounted for dangerman Ian Botham's wicket on three occasions, often playing on the all-rounder's impetuosity with unerring accuracy, Fowler also three times, as well as England skipper David Gower and their most in-form batsman Allan Lamb. So no cheap wickets. No tailender lobbing it up to mid-off. Baptiste knew his role was to frustrate the English top-order batsmen and he did not disappoint his captain.

'The other guys were quicker than I was, but I had a different set of skills,' Baptiste admitted. 'They might bowl you 15 overs and take 4-60 but I could bowl longer spells and maybe go for less runs. I never tried to be like them, I knew what I was and what I could do. I could bowl long spells if that was what the captain wanted from me and I would generally keep things tight, hitting my lines and lengths.'

His figures at Lord's, for instance, read 20-6-36-2 in the first innings and he again went at less than two runs per over in his 26 overs in the second innings. His teammates, and especially his captain, were grateful for that control he offered while the quicker bowlers were rotated.

'He played his role tremendously well and probably didn't get the credit he deserved,' said Courtney Walsh, who sat on the sidelines for all five Tests on the tour. 'He wasn't super-fast, but he could contain batsmen and that's what they needed, someone to play that role, be consistent, bowl long spells and chip in with the bat, too.'

England all-rounder Derek Pringle accepted that Baptiste 'was probably underrated' though England would not have been doubting his ability when he helped to set a ruthless tone for the series at Edgbaston in the first Test, when scoring a Test career best of 87 not out. It was one of several key contributions, like his 44 at Lord's that helped the West Indies to reduce their first-innings deficit.

'Eldine was a very talented all-rounder and had great determination,' Jeffrey Dujon said. 'He did what he was asked to do with the ball and his batting gave us a bit more depth, too. I generally batted at six or seven and having Eldine down there in the lower order gave me more freedom to play my shots. He was a key man and performed his role very well.'

That he remained at Kent from 1981 through to 1987, impressing with consistent performances rather than the spectacular, summed up his character and key asset of reliability.

Fast bowler Winston Davis was unlucky not to make the original tour squad, as Walsh and Milton Small were chosen as backup. Aged 25 and approaching his prime, Davis had taken a record 33 wickets in the domestic Shell Shield competition in the 1982/83 campaign that initially brought him West Indies recognition in the shape of selection for the 1983 World Cup in England, and subsequently a Test tour of India later that year. The World Cup fast-tracked him on to cricket's proverbial map globally, for his 7-51 against Australia at Headingley brought him notoriety. He had also become a county player with Glamorgan by then.

Gaining selection to the West Indies team for a fast bowler in the 1980s was challenging enough. Davis, though, was well accustomed to fighting his corner and scrapping for opportunities for he was one of seven boys in his family, who all played either football or cricket. He impressed youth talent scouts enough in St Vincent to win selection to the West Indies under-19 team that toured England in 1976, while aged 17. He took his chance, dismissing David Gower, Mike Gatting and Paul Downton in his first-innings 4-35, and added Bill Athey in the second innings. A promising career developed from there and, by 1983, he was playing for the West Indies alongside fast bowlers regarded as worldwide legends.

Davis humbly accepted his place on the rich assembly line of West Indian fast bowlers and was realistic about his chances of becoming established.

'The West Indies had tremendous fast-bowling material and there were plenty of quality bowlers who could have played more international cricket,' Davis said. 'When you think there was Marshall, Garner, Holding and Roberts, it was difficult to remove them. If they were fit, it's obvious they were going to play 90-something per cent of the time.

'Still, I was disappointed not to get the call at times when I felt I deserved to. I had a great tour to India but the way I bowled wasn't reflected with a big haul of wickets. I was able to unsettle many of the Indian batsmen on, supposedly, slow pitches. I didn't find the pitches as slow as they made out.'

Once Andy Roberts left the team Davis might have expected to become the next incumbent in the famous pace quartet, but in came Baptiste instead. (In no particular order) then Courtney Walsh, then Tony Gray, Patrick Patterson, Winston Benjamin, Curtly Ambrose and Ian Bishop, right through to the end of the 1980s. Davis was surprised not to have been called up more for the West Indies and played just 15 Tests in a career spanning five years.

'I was certainly disappointed not to get the call-up in the first place for the 1984 tour, and then to be dropped after the New Zealand series in '85,' Davis reflected. 'But ultimately I was a professional and you soon get over these things by getting work elsewhere such as Glamorgan, Tasmania, Wellington and Northamptonshire.'

Davis played just the fourth Test in the '84 series having replaced Milton Small in the squad, but still made a telling impact, with his enthralling 77 as nightwatchman at Old Trafford, which helped to take the game further away from England.

He had already shown that summer prior to his call-up that he could bat with scores of 22 not out and 41 not out when following on for Glamorgan against Middlesex, who fielded an attack consisting of Wayne Daniel, Norman Cowans, Neil Williams, John Emburey and Phil Edmonds.

Famously, Davis also broke Paul Terry's arm with an awkward short ball. England opener Chris Broad suggested Davis had a bowling action reminiscent of current England quick Jofra Archer, as he had a very short run-up with a quick and explosive arm action. 'He would surprise you with his pace,' said Broad.

David Gower added: 'Winnie was sharp and a good example of how well off the West Indies were for pace-bowling talent. They could have picked any one from ten or 15 and they wouldn't have been much weaker for it. He had a beanpole figure, good height, with whippy pace – nothing came easy from any of those guys.'

On his distinctive short run-up and action, Davis explained: 'I started off with a 22-yard run-up, but I cut it down to 15 yards. We were in Australia playing a one-day series and I had hurt my hamstring. While I was recovering Malcolm Marshall got injured on the morning of a match against Pakistan at Brisbane and Clive asked me if I would be fit enough to play. I said, "Yes, no problem," and bowled off 15 yards and it was one of the quickest spells I ever bowled so I stuck with my short run-up after that.'

The position of Roger Harper in the West Indies team in the 1980s might seem to have been something of a luxury to the casual observer. But if you asked captain Clive Lloyd you would have received a very different answer. Lloyd regarded Harper as a crucial figure to their dominance in 1984 and indeed to their squad, with his underrated and accurate off-spinners, his useful middle-order runs, and especially his scintillating fielding, whether swooping and throwing at the stumps or catching in the slips or covers.

Harper announced himself to English audiences right from his first international appearance of that summer, at Lord's in the third ODI when he ran out Allan Lamb for a first-ball duck off his own bowling. It was the type of slick fielding that quickly established him unofficially as the undisputed best fielder in the world, probably of the decade. If Colin Bland revolutionised fielding in the sixties, and Clive Lloyd and Derek Randall took on that baton through the seventies and early eighties, Harper owned the eighties, before Jonty Rhodes and Herschelle Gibbs took fielding standards on to new levels from the 1990s. Harper's run-out of Graham Gooch in the Lord's Bicentenary match in 1987 was another example of what he was capable of. Gooch, with 117 to his name, drove firmly down the pitch, before Harper's pick-up and throw at the stumps had Gooch scrambling well short of his ground, to be the latest victim of cricket's champion gunslinger.

At 6ft 4½in, Harper wasn't your average low-to-the-ground swooper. But he was lithe and agile, which had been assets he possessed since his formative years. As a child in Guyana, he played athletics, basketball, table tennis, football 'and I even joined in with the girls who did hopscotch and skipping, too', Harper recalled with a smile. 'All those things helped with my agility and athleticism.'

This background was also central to his fielding development, which he began to enjoy from an early age.

'My brother (former first-class player, Mark) is almost six years older than me, and was cricket crazy and I followed him around,' Harper recalled. 'Whether it was on the side of the ground at matches or in my cousin's yard, I always hung around with the big boys who were all older than me. Therefore, I didn't get a chance to bat too often so I had to field most of the time. If you wanted to carry on playing with the big boys you couldn't complain so I would put myself in a position where the ball would go often so at least I was busy.

'At the time I was just having fun, but without realising it I was developing and honing my fielding skills which prepared me for my cricket later in life.'

Harper, like Baptiste, was an integral member of the West Indies team in 1984 yet could also be unappreciated and underrated by those out of the inner circle who did not understand his worth to the side. Clearly, he was an off-spinner in a team synonymous with bowlers delivering the ball at frightening pace and was therefore something of an outlier.

'We didn't know him when he came to Taunton for the tour game in May,' recalled Somerset's stand-in skipper Vic Marks. 'We saw this 6ft 5in fellow, a fantastic athlete, and were incredibly relieved when he started to bowl off-breaks. And yet he still took five wickets!' (5-32.)

One of the reasons captain Lloyd appreciated Harper was not because of his all-round skills with bat, ball or in the field, but his attitude. Harper totally bought into the role he was expected to perform. He knew the West Indies would invariably bowl teams out with their fast bowlers but once in a while, he would be called upon to exploit a wearing, turning pitch, like at Old Trafford, or even just to keep an end tight while Lloyd rested Marshall, Garner and Holding. Like Baptiste, who was also adept at that supporting role, Harper strengthened the batting.

'The thing is this, I came into a team where the fast bowlers were dominating games over a long period already, so, there was no need for me to be crying in the corner, it was more about how I could contribute to make the team better,' Harper said. 'There were some Tests where I might have just five or six overs in the match and sometimes not in an innings at all. But that was what was required.

'I had played in the series against Australia in the Caribbean but then going to England I knew the conditions would mainly favour the fast bowlers, especially when it was overcast. The captain wanted to ensure there was balance in the team and so kept his options open. By using Baptiste and myself we had great depth in our batting, and we were able to back up the fast bowlers as well.'

Harper impressed so much throughout that 1984 tour that he earned himself a county contract to play at Northamptonshire, where he played from 1985/87.

Lancashire's Jack Simmons brokered the contract, on the recommendation of his county team-mate Lloyd.

Northants team-mate Allan Lamb appreciated what Harper brought to the Wantage Road county and felt he 'turned it quite a bit' as a spinner.

David Gower also regarded Harper as being a better cricketer than he may well have been given credit for, such was the attention on the fast bowlers and flamboyant batsmen in the team.

'His role was so often to just fill in a few overs,' Gower said. 'I quite liked his action, there was something graceful about it. He didn't have much of a run-up, just a high jump and got a bit of drift. He was also an outstanding fielder. Clive must have handled him well as someone like Harper would have had to understand his role in the team was going to be limited and accept that whatever you're asked to do, do it to the best of your ability which he did.'

Also unheralded on the 1984 tour were the support players who were there to play in all the many county games, gaining valuable experience in English conditions and ready to return four years later and be all the better for their exposure.

Courtney Walsh, Milton Small, Gus Logie, Richie Richardson and deputy wicketkeeper-batsman Thelston Payne had to remain patient on long tours like this one to England, where their roles were predominantly about development than rather playing in the main theatres and taking central roles in the Tests.

They generally understood what their jobs were, but it still did not mean they were happy to sit on the sidelines during Test matches and take no part other than to ferry drinks. Lloyd would have wanted nothing different but young players with good attitudes on the fringes desperate to be a part of the team, and hungry to break into the side.

'I was disappointed not to play any Test cricket on that tour,' Walsh admitted. 'But I was a rookie, and my role was to play the side games and just make sure I learnt from the senior guys as much as I could. To watch the quality of cricket they played, the never-say-die attitude they showed, the confidence they had to always get the job done was something extra special.

'Michael Holding was my roommate for my first two tours, before Malcolm Marshall, so I was never short on good advice.'

Terry's Sad Farewell

'Bad judgement is usually the reason for batsmen getting hit and if they do get into a tangle, a cricket ball travelling at 90 to 95 miles per hour can do a lot of damage.' – Winston Davis

Things were going so well for Hampshire batsman Paul Terry. Runs, lots of them and against quality bowlers, and then an England call-up and a Test debut against the West Indies at Leeds. Sadly, his career was soon to take a turn for the worse.

Within three weeks in July, Terry's international career had been and gone. Not that he knew it then, but that was to be it. And as if his struggle with the bat wasn't bad enough, he sustained an injury that would keep him out of cricket for eight months.

First the good news. Terry plundered three County Championship centuries in four games before his Test debut – 102 against Surrey and their chief destroyer Sylvester Clarke; 136 against South African quick Garth Le Roux and his Sussex team; and then 175 not out versus Gloucestershire and their new-ball duo John Shepherd and David Lawrence.

'I don't remember the exact figures, but I know I was in good form before my Test debut,' Terry acknowledged. 'I had only just established myself in the Hampshire team towards the back end of the '83 season so things started to happen quickly for me.'

The England selectors drafted Terry in after three other batsmen had needed to be replaced after just two Tests, with the injured Andy Lloyd being a forced change, and Derek Randall and Mike Gatting's form having not instilled confidence that they would succeed in the series.

'We were casting around looking for someone to play that (number three) role,' David Gower said. 'Paul was a bloody good player. He scored a stack of runs at Hampshire when I was there a few years later, and he was a brilliant fielder who made catches look easy at slip.'

The Terry that Gower was describing, though, was probably more the 1990s version, as the player himself was not even confident in his own ability to play Test cricket in 1984. By the time of the third Test he soon found out if he had the temperament to survive.

A nervous Terry occupied the crease for just over half an hour after Gower won the toss and elected to bat. He saw Graeme Fowler depart quickly and he walked to the wicket at number three to join Chris Broad. They put on 30 but he never felt comfortable before edging to Roger Harper off Michael Holding for 8. The second innings was worse, lbw Garner for 1 from eight nerve-wracking deliveries.

'I was never an overly confident sort of guy,' Terry said, 'and that lack of confidence probably held me back throughout my career. I never had the confidence and belief in myself that the top players had. I remember being very nervous when I went out to bat. My Hampshire team-mate Gordon Greenidge came up to me while I was taking my guard and he wished me well, which was a nice touch.

'After I got out, I watched my dismissal on the TV replay. It just didn't look like me. My footwork was terrible, and the nerves had clearly got to me. It was an up and down pitch but mentally I just wasn't up for it.'

That difficult beginning was about to get a whole lot worse. There were two List A games back at his county which didn't bring any runs or much-needed confidence before he met up with his England colleagues for the fourth Test in Manchester.

He was bowled by Kent's Australian overseas player Terry Alderman for a duck in a NatWest Trophy second round match at Southampton, before missing out against Yorkshire in the John Player Special Sunday League at Bournemouth. Not the kind of preparation he would have wanted before another opportunity to prolong his Test career against the West Indies.

This time Clive Lloyd won the toss and opted to bat on his home ground where he had played since 1968. West Indies were all out for 500 on the stroke of stumps and Terry knew he would almost certainly be batting the next day, on the Saturday.

Fowler and Broad kept him waiting anxiously in the dressing room with an opening partnership of 90, before Fowler's dismissal. Terry then scrapped his way to 7, when the fate of his England career was sealed courtesy of a short ball from Winston Davis.

'It just didn't bounce as much as I expected,' Terry recalled. 'I wasn't wearing an arm guard, and my natural reaction was to protect my head with my wrist. If I was wearing an arm guard, I would have been fine, but I had never worn one. I just never felt the need to put one on, though I always wore one afterwards.

'I remember getting hit on my arm a few times weeks earlier to Sylvester Clarke, but I must have been struck on the fleshy part then. This time I was hit smack on the bone – and it did me serious damage.'

X-rays revealed Terry had broken his left ulna. His arm was in a cast for 18 weeks and he was out of action until February the following year, when he toured Zimbabwe with England A.

'Funnily enough I went into this game feeling much more confident because I'd hit a lot of balls in the lead-up,' Terry added. 'Foxy and Broady were hit a few times before I went in, so it wasn't the easiest batting conditions.' (Davis hit Fowler on the back of his helmet with a bouncer that never got up.)

It was clear Marshall would return for the fifth Test, so Davis was intent on making a positive impression with such competition among the West Indian pace bowlers. Davis did not try to injure Terry but maintained such dangers went with the territory of playing against the West Indies.

'Fast, short-pitched deliveries are uncomfortable, if well directed,' Davis commented. 'I never set out to hurt batsmen, and they only tended to get hit when they made a mistake, like not getting out of the way when they should or not reading the bounce correctly.

'Bad judgement is usually the reason for batsmen getting hit and if they do get into a tangle, a cricket ball travelling at 90 to 95 miles per hour can do a lot of damage. And yes, people have been struck, unfortunately.'

Terry thought his Test match was over once he had been treated at hospital and told that he should not go anywhere near a cricket pitch for several weeks at least.

But then circumstances presented themselves that meant Terry would be required to bat with his left arm tucked under his jumper in a sling, having been in hospital the day before.

Allan Lamb was 98 not out and approaching a third Test century in as many matches when it looked as though he would be stranded on the fall of the ninth wicket.

'The communication from the captain wasn't great,' Terry recalled. 'We were seven wickets down and 22 runs from avoiding the follow-on and I was sitting in the changing room in my civvies. There had been no discussion at all about me going out to bat. Then suddenly it was all very hurried as Pat Pocock and Norman Cowans got out quickly, and I was asked to go out and bat to help Lamby reach his hundred.

'I had a cast on from my wrist to my shoulder and it was like a military operation to help me get into my whites and padded up because I couldn't do anything for myself. The lads helped me get dressed and padded up. My memory of who did what to help me is cloudy because I was drugged up at the time as I was in so much pain.

'Once Lamby scored the two runs he needed to get to his century, he thought that was it and started to walk off, but we were waved at to stay out there and bat on from everyone on the balcony. We were still 20 runs from avoiding the follow-on.

'So, I had to face Joel Garner's 90-miles-per-hour thunderbolts while I was pretty drugged up. He missed my stumps with an attempted yorker first ball but got me next ball as I backed away quite a lot as I didn't wish to get hit again given the state that I was already in.'

Lamb did not want or expect to stay out on the ground once he had reached three figures as he was aware of the considerable pain Terry was experiencing just by running between the wickets, as his broken bone jarred with every stride.

'Once I got the two runs we started walking off, but David told us to stay,' Lamb said. 'That was a ridiculous, stupid decision from David, making Terry face Joel Garner with one arm. The communication was terrible. What they were doing sending out Terry I'll never know.'

Gower, for his part, accepts he did not deal with the situation very well, but it is seemingly yet another example of how a captain – and an inexperienced one here after all – can think when they are being pushed to their limits by such a dominant team.

'I felt sorry for Paul for breaking his arm in the first place,' Gower said. 'I kind of regret sending him out at the end of the innings with a broken arm. To be fair to Paul, he probably did mind going out, but he didn't show it.

'The initial idea was to help Lamby get to three figures but keeping him out there was a bit of a desperate move and didn't feel right when I reflected on it.'

The Oval Chronicles, Fifth Test

Lloyd's Clean Sweep!

'All of their guys had tremendous respect for their captain and anyone that came into the team had this same overwhelming respect for Clive.' – Allan Lamb

England succumbed to their first whitewash at home in Test cricket in over a hundred years of contests, as Clive Lloyd's West Indies completed what seemed an almost inevitable scoreline of 5-0 at The Oval, the fifth such occasion in a five-match series.

How fitting it was that Lloyd, three weeks before his 40th birthday, was the man who bailed his team out of trouble in the first innings with 60 not out to ensure they went on to a comfortable victory in what was his 20th and final Test match in England. One more series, one more challenge, lay ahead for him in Australia, but he was almost done.

Lloyd, who recovered from a viral infection to take his place in the match, proved that he was far from washed up as a batsman or captain, ending the series with an average of 51 and helping to read England their last rites.

It was also a match in which Michael Holding rolled back the years to revert to his long run on what was the quickest pitch of the series, almost in homage to his 14-wicket career highlight on the same ground in 1976. This match also saw opener Desmond Haynes finally demonstrate the kind of form that had been expected of him all summer, as he contributed a man-of-the-match innings of 125 in the second innings.

Set 375 to win, England were bowled out for 202 in their second innings as Holding (5-43) and Joel Garner (4-51) steamrolled Gower's shell-shocked, battered and bruised men for the final time of the summer. 'We lost 5-0 but we had our moments, and we just weren't good enough to take our chances when those opportunities presented themselves,' Chris Broad acknowledged.

The occasion, though, belonged to Lloyd. At the completion to this match, he had led the West Indies in 69 Tests and in his last 36 had lost just once, in Melbourne. Not a bad record from the man who was almost certainly the greatest leader in their history. Some may offer Frank Worrell's name but results would suggest Lloyd would be hard to overlook. Eldine Baptiste even suggested Lloyd's batting was still good enough at this point for a further two years of Test cricket, but he had almost had enough.

'All of their guys had tremendous respect for their captain and anyone that came into the team had this same overwhelming respect for Clive,' Allan Lamb observed. 'They were all disciplined professionals – nobody stepped out of line.'

Lloyd was the first West Indies captain to win Test series in Australia and Pakistan and of course to orchestrate this whitewash of England. Some critics who were less complimentary of Lloyd as a captain suggested he wasn't a great tactician and relied entirely on 'blasting out' opponents with the formidable pace attack that he had at his disposal. But it was Lloyd, of course, who opted to go in this direction and exploit the strength of the pace-bowling battery.

Lloyd the batsman, though, did all he could to achieve superiority at The Oval after winning the toss and electing to bat first. He soon looked on with disbelief when his team were reduced to 70/6 against an England that had given debuts to two seamers – Richard Ellison and Jonathan Agnew.

'I had seen that before from Clive,' David Gower commented. 'On our previous tour to the Caribbean under Beefy, Clive had played those kinds of innings.' (He scored 100 in Barbados when they were 65/4.)

Jeffrey Dujon added: 'Even then, coming towards the end of his career, Clive was still a force to be reckoned with, with the bat. He was a good leader, a pretty calm individual, which you need when you're under pressure, and he showed these qualities in that innings.'

Ian Botham's 5-72 caused most of the damage and the wicket of Dujon saw him become the third Englishman to 300 Test wickets after Fred Trueman and Bob Willis. There had been some calls for him to be omitted from the team following his earlier statement that he would be skipping the winter tour of India. The selectors, though, did not wish to be without him while trying to stave off a whitewash.

If England had been able to prevent the ever-reliable Baptiste from batting for over an hour with Lloyd for his 32, who knows how England might have responded. Instead, the tourists stretched their total to 190 before knocking England over for just 162, largely on the back of another inspired spell from Malcolm Marshall (5-35). Graeme Fowler had to retire hurt when on 12 after a Marshall bouncer struck his arm.

Haynes was averaging just 15.71 in the series before opening up his second innings of the Test and was probably the one man in the West Indies line-up who had underachieved that summer. Even in the Texaco Trophy matches he had only registered 1, 4 and 18. But as great players often do, he made the most of his final Test match opportunity of the tour by registering his seventh century, of what would be a total of 18 by his retirement. It was a more extreme example of his tour in 1980 when he scored 184 at Lord's but was otherwise unspectacular.

England's second innings was dominated by Holding and Garner, who were three years out from their eventual retirements. Holding took 3-5 in an explosive 17-ball spell as he removed Broad, Gower and Lamb.

Holding underwent knee cartilage surgery in February 1982 and thereafter lost confidence about running in hard and bowling fast. He was tentative about slamming his foot down on delivery. He was still effective and was happy enough with his game, mentally and physically, but was slightly tentative at letting rip like he used to, a la Barbados 1981 and The Oval 1976.

Andy Roberts knew Holding's bowling better than anyone. They had not only been team-mates since 1975 but were also roommates and shared huge mutual respect. When on tour to India in 1983, Roberts spotted this hesitance from his buddy and suggested to Holding that he shorten his run-up.

Holding was reluctant at first but eventually put Roberts' idea to the test after he received skipper Lloyd's blessing. Very quickly he realised he was still bowling sharply but without so much extra strain on his body. But after tea on the fourth day at The Oval, he felt it was time to give a nod to his former glories of eight years earlier by coming in off his old long run. He never disappointed.

'Mikey bowled well,' Allan Lamb recalled. 'He was still able to turn it on by '84, and really steamed in off his long run. He wasn't a big swinger of the ball, just had pace and hit the seam quite often.'

Broad remembers the moment when Holding felt it was time to abandon his short run and give his long run another try.

'After Chris Tavare and I had put on a partnership (of 60), Mikey had clearly had enough because he walked past his usual run-up mark and went back to his full run,' Broad recalled. 'He then bowled me this bouncer that I just didn't see, it smacked me on the glove and looped to Greenidge in the gully. It was a lot quicker than any other ball I had faced in that innings.

'I always knew all their bowlers had a delivery up their sleeve that was quicker than their average ball that they could bowl at any time. You just had to hope you got out of the way of it or that it passed you by.

'I would not have liked to face Michael Holding in his heyday in '76 and '81 because he was quick enough in '84. He wasn't at full throttle all the time, but he was still a force to be reckoned with and every now and again he would let you know he was still one of the greatest fast bowlers in the world.'

Gower had experienced Holding previously at his most hostile in 1981 in the Caribbean so knew what he was capable of. It was of little surprise to him when Holding came steaming in.

'It's all relative,' Gower said. 'Look at Botham, even when he lost his pace, he still conned people out. If you had Michael Holding at 80 per cent, as a batsman you're still looking for the ball when he bowls at a hundred per cent. You're wary of going, "Oh, he's knackered." At The Oval he was still able to bowl quick and straight and full and could still hit you on the pad and get you lbw. He was far from a spent force.'

England debutant Richard Ellison, known for swinging the ball away from the right-hander prodigiously when at his best, had enough of a promising debut to earn himself selection in the Sri Lanka Test at Lord's later that month, followed by a place on the India tour and then the series for which he is better known, the Ashes in 1985. He only played 11 Tests all told in his career, but he never let anyone down.

He took five wickets on his Test debut (and still has the ball with which he claimed his first Test wicket, Larry

Gomes caught by Ian Botham), and batted for 77 minutes for 20 not out in England's first innings.

'Facing these blokes was about survival for me,' left-handed batsman and right-arm bowler Ellison said. 'Ducking and weaving and staying out there. It was about hanging around for as long as I could because I wasn't a Graham Gooch, a David Gower or Allan Lamb. Chris Tavare pushed me up the order at Kent, so I was often batting at six and seven above Alan Knott and Graham Johnson. That stood me in good stead for Test cricket.'

Ellison's fellow debutant Agnew only took two wickets but what two wickets they were! Gordon Greenidge caught at slip by Botham and Viv Richards lbw for 15.

'In different circumstances,' Gower said, 'Aggers might well have played a few more Test matches (than his three). As for Elli, he had a real good 12 months.'

Ellison paid tribute to Australian swing bowler Terry Alderman, who was his team-mate at Kent, for offering lots of good advice about creating more professional habits around his cricket. Alderman played at Canterbury in 1984 and 1986 and encouraged Ellison to have a positive attitude towards fitness – when he was able to.

'Terry had a big influence on me,' Ellison enthused. 'If we didn't play much and were stuck in the pavilion all day, we might run around the ground ten times, or do stretches. That was how I started to go about my cricket.

'So, on the morning of my Test debut, Terry's example was still fresh in my head and as I prepared to do my three laps around the ground, I couldn't find my trainers. I was changing next to Ian Botham, who was a hero of mine, and I didn't say too much to him at first. I then found out why he was known to be something of a pest in the dressing room when it was pointed out to me that my trainers had been superglued to the ceiling. That was my first experience of changing next to Ian Botham!'

If Ellison's career was starting to take off, Tavare's was heading in the opposite direction. This match was his first opportunity of the summer and he seemed to cope well, adding grit and determination to England's batting at number three with his innings of 49 made in over three hours. It earned a place in the Sri Lanka Test but there at Lord's he stonewalled 14 runs in 95 balls and didn't play again for five years, with one more match against Australia.

'We know the riddle that is Tav,' Gower said. 'For Kent he was free-scoring; for England his role was different and it took all his resolve and concentration to play in a more defensive manner but it was felt that was what was needed. I don't know whether he thinks back and wonders whether he should have been a bit more like his true self as he was with Kent.

'I certainly didn't give him any instructions in '84. In '81, Beefy smashed it all around and Tav held up the other end. In those days you were allowed to have a mix. Bazball now is bonkers because no one is allowed to play the anchor innings.'

Comically, though it was no laughing matter at the time, Ellison told a story of how last batsman Agnew was forced to run off the ground at the time of West Indies' historic victory while being mugged of all his kit. Clearly, among the many West Indian spectators running on to the outfield, there were those who wanted their piece of memorabilia to mark the occasion.

'Aggers, who I was batting with at the end, got back into the changing room and he didn't have a piece of kit left that he went out to bat with,' Ellison said with a smile. 'The crowds had ran on and just got what they could in their jubilation to celebrate the 5-0. Jonathan arrived back in the changing room and said, "They've taken everything!" His pads, gloves, helmet, his bat, was all gone.'

It is only right the final word on the outcome of the series should go to one of the West Indies legends who had such influence on the proceedings. Malcolm Marshall, who sadly passed away due to cancer when aged 41 in 1999, took aim at England's wayward bowlers for not helping to make it a more competitive series.

'When the game's historians look back on that first "blackwash", a comprehensive 5-0 thrashing, they will point to the mastery of the West Indian fast bowlers,' Marshall reflected. 'Of course we played our part, but in my view, it was the failure of the England bowlers and the indifference of the fielding which was the main reason for their failure to at least reduce the margin of defeat.

'I realise they never had the bowlers to match our pace, however most of the Test wickets were not particularly helpful to us. They were made for the medium-pacer who could get a bit of movement and take advantage of the variation in bounce. The England bowlers failed to do this and allowed themselves to be steamrollered even when the conditions suited them better than us. It was the England bowlers who lost the series for them, not the batsmen.'

THE OVAL SCORECARD

West Indies

	First Innings		Second Innings:	
C.G. Greenidge	lbw b Botham	22	c Botham b Agnew	34
D.L. Haynes	b Allott	10	b Botham	125
H.A. Gomes	c Botham b Ellison	18	c Tavare b Ellison	1
I.V.A. Richards	c Allott b Botham	8	lbw b Agnew	15
P.J. Dujon	c Tavare b Botham	3	(6) c Lamb b Ellison	49
C.H. Lloyd	not out	60	(5) c Downton b Ellison	36
M.D. Marshall	c Gower b Ellison	0	(8) c Lamb b Botham	12
E.A.E. Baptiste	c Fowler b Allott	32	(7) c Downton b Allott	5
R.A. Harper	b Botham	18	c Downton b Allott	17
M.A. Holding	lbw b Botham	0	lbw b Botham	30
J. Garner	c Downton b Allott	6	not out	10
70 overs, 13 extras		190	96.3 overs, 12 extras.	346

Fall of wickets 1st Innings: 1-19 (Haynes); 2-45 (Greenidge); 3-64 (Gomes); 4-64 (Richards); 5-67 (Dujon); 6-70 (Marshall); 7-124 (Baptiste); 8-154 (Harper); 9-154 (Holding); 10-190 (Garner)

Bowling: Agnew 12-3-46-0; Allott 17-7-25-3; Botham 23-8-72-5; Ellison 18-3-34-2

Fall of wickets 2nd Innings: 1-51 (Greenidge); 2-52 (Gomes); 3-69 (Richards); 4-132 (Lloyd); 5-214 (Dujon); 6-237 (Baptiste); 7-264 (Marshall); 8-293 (Harper); 9-329 (Haynes); 10-346 (Holding)

Bowling: Agnew 14-1-51-2; Allott 26-1-96-2; Botham 22.3-2-103-3; Ellison 26-7-60-3; Pocock 8-3-24-0

England

	First Innings		Second Innings	
G. Fowler	c Richards b Baptiste	31	c Richards b Marshall	7
B.C. Broad	b Garner	4	c Greenidge b Holding	39
P.I. Pocock	c Greenidge b Marshall	0	(10) c & b Holding	0
C.J. Tavare	c Dujon b Holding	16	(3) c Richards b Garner	49
D.I. Gower	c Dujon b Holding	12	(4) lbw b Holding	7
A.J. Lamb	lbw b Marshall	12	(5) c Haynes b Holding	1
I.T. Botham	c Dujon b Marshall	14	(6) c Marshall b Garner	54
P.R. Downton	c Lloyd b Garner	16	(7) lbw b Garner	10
R.M. Ellison	not out	20	(8) c Holding b Garner	13
P.J.W. Allott	b Marshall	16	(9) c Lloyd b Holding	4
J.P. Agnew	b Marshall	5	not out	2
61.5 overs, 16 extras		162	69.4 overs, 16 extras	202

Fall of wickets 1st Innings: 1-10 (Broad); 1-21 (Fowler retired hurt); 2-22 (Pocock); 3-45 (Gower); 4-64 (Tavare); 5-83 (Botham); 6-84 (Lamb); 7-116 (Fowler); 8-133 (Downton); 9-156 (Allott); 10-162 (Agnew)

Bowling: Garner 18-6-37-2; Marshall 17.5-5-35-5; Holding 13-2-55-2; Baptiste 12-4-19-1; Harper 1-1-0-0

Fall of wickets 2nd Innings: 1-15 (Fowler); 2-75 (Broad); 3-88 (Gower); 4-90 (Lamb); 5-135 (Tavare); 6-181 (Botham); 7-186 (Downton); 8-200 (Allott); 9-200 (Pocock); 10-202 (Ellison)

Toss: West Indies, elected to bat first

Player of the match: Desmond Haynes

Player of the series: Gordon Greenidge

West Indies won by 172 runs

Gower's Misery

'He didn't look the same player that I had seen before, and after. Maybe the pressures of captaincy for the first time weighed on his mind. He was a quality player so the level of expectation on him to deliver against us would have taken its toll.' – Jeffrey Dujon

Clive Lloyd wrote in a newspaper column in 1982 that David Gower should have been installed as the new England captain that summer as the successor to Keith Fletcher and ahead of fellow candidate Bob Willis, who was eventually handed the reins.

Lloyd felt it was the wrong call and that Gower should have been given the six home Tests against India and Pakistan in which to pave the way for the winter tour to Australia and develop some confidence as the leader of the team in a less pressurised environment.

'They have made the mistake of picking a stop-gap captain and robbed Gower of any chance of learning his job in easy conditions,' Lloyd wrote. 'That way there would not have been the pressure on him as there was with Ian Botham when he began against West Indies and Australia.'

Hindsight would suggest that Lloyd was correct. Willis wasn't a *dreadful* captain, but the point is that England had an opportunity to expose the younger, forward-looking option of Gower and missed their chance.

Instead, like Botham before him in 1980, Gower had the unenviable task of trying to beat – or even compete with – the world-leading West Indies in a five-match Test series first up. That England lost 5-0 didn't reflect well on Gower's initial captaincy reputation, but realistic observers would have sympathised with his plight, even if he did struggle to adjust to the steep challenge.

Australian great Bobby Simpson once said that a captain is only as good as his bowling attack and Gower's was considerably inferior to what Lloyd had at his disposal.

'Nobody is a ready-made captain, you have to learn on the job, and when things are not going your way and are as tough as they were in 1984 against the best team that possibly ever played the game, you have to find a way,' Gower reflected. 'That is made even more difficult when you're a batsman and not scoring the runs you'd like to.

'I had support from Bob, but it was clear he was running out of steam and wasn't going to last the series; Beefy (Ian Botham) was supportive but was still Beefy being Beefy. Your progress is also partly determined by how much leeway you're given by the opposition and how quickly you learn on the job, and when you're getting hammered consistently it's tough. They always tried to destabilise the captain, too, so I had to dig a bit deeper.'

Several elements went against Gower such as injuries and the missing rebels – there can be little doubt that his team would have been more competitive with Graham Gooch, John Emburey, possibly Derek Underwood and definitely the young paceman Graham Dilley, who was enduring a nightmare run of injuries at that time. Dilley's extra firepower may have made a difference at those times when West Indies had lost early wickets but managed to recover.

The injuries in the series to Andy Lloyd and Paul Terry would have had a destabilising effect on his team and selection, while he was also let down by the sudden decline or ongoing failures of his senior players such as Willis, Derek Randall, Mike Gatting, Geoff Miller and Botham – who continued to struggle against the West Indies in a way that he never did against other main rivals Australia.

'It wasn't as bad as the blind leading the blind,' Gower said dryly, 'but this was a difficult series for the selectors when you consider the circumstances, the results, the injuries, absentees. All these things add up and unless you're competitive in matches, which, by definition, means more players are in decent form, there's less chance of keeping the same XI going.'

Another aspect central to Gower's misery was his own lack of runs. He amassed just 171 at an average of 19 in ten innings.

Something a batting captain wants to do when his team is down and defeated is at least show strong leadership by leading from the front with an impressive return of Test match runs, as Allan Border managed to do as Australia's new skipper later in 1984. Australia were losing badly, but Border stood firm and resisted like a true warrior.

Jeffrey Dujon stood behind every one of Gower's deliveries in that 1984 series and he felt Gower was not at his best all summer because of the added stresses of captaincy against a top quality team.

'David had made a lot of runs in the Caribbean, before my time (in 1980/81),' Dujon said. 'So, we were aware of his threat. He didn't really have a lot of footwork to start with. We looked to stay on or around his off stump. He was a fine player, there was no question about that, but he never really got going. To me it never looked like his heart was in it. David is a very laid-back kind of fella anyway and is somebody who I know well, but he never had that. I'm not sure if it's desire, but he lost a step or two in that series.

'He didn't look the same player that I had seen before, and after. Maybe the pressures of captaincy for the first time weighed on his mind. He was a quality player so the level of expectation on him to deliver against us would have taken its toll.'

Gower's so-called vulnerability outside off stump and his tendency to chase balls he should leave alone is not an accusation that he wouldn't have heard a great many times. We have to accept the failures as much as we should glory in the good days of his kind of player, the majestic stroke-players that we have seen before and after his time like

Ted Dexter, Carl Hooper, Mark Waugh and maybe even Kevin Pietersen. But Gower did frustrate because he was such a wonderfully talented batsman.

'Gower is without doubt a world-class batsman,' New Zealand fast-bowling legend Richard Hadlee wrote in his book *At the Double* in the 1980s. 'He has a ton of time in which to play the ball and if you bowl straight at him or stray a little down the leg side, you'll get hit. The same if you drop too short.

'But for a batsman of his class, he has a weakness on or outside the off stump. To be fair, many players are weak in that area, but Gower gives the impression of being very casual and loose, especially early in the innings. After an initial run of success, teams have worked him out and know exactly where to bowl to him. You fill the off side with three slips and two gullies and if you're good enough and consistent enough to bowl around off stump, he'll play and miss and eventually get out. The number of times he's caught in the area is incredible.'

You could find as many ex-players to be openly complimentary of Gower's class as Hadlee was measured in his praise. Malcolm Marshall once selected Gower in his World XI that he insisted had to be devoid of West Indians otherwise his whole XI would be West Indian.

Gower's statistics were certainly curious against the West Indies. His average of 43.88 against Clive Lloyd's team in the Caribbean, on those bouncy, sometimes lightning quick, pitches reflects a batsman who clearly had a great amount of time and no doubt much ability to play hostile pace bowling. Yet his average of 22.38 against the West Indies in England does create some bemusement for a player of his quality.

There will be lots of reasons, such as the sudden pressure of captaincy in 1984, but the two-paced wickets probably did not always encourage fluent strokeplay against some of the best fast bowlers the game has seen. Good batsmen usually find a way to cope with extreme pace, but when you cannot be sure of the bounce, that challenge becomes extra-difficult.

'These quirks are what keep statisticians in jobs,' Gower said. 'In the West Indies the pitches were fast and bouncy, less sideways movement, and generally I didn't do badly on quicker pitches.

'Ultimately, in this series I was struggling. But throughout my main period of captaincy from '84 to '86 I went through pretty much every sequence of form and scenario. In India in 1984/85 we won the series and I didn't get enough runs, in '85 against Australia we won the series and I scored lots of runs, then we lost another series in the West Indies when I was pretty competitive with the bat, so it depends how people want to interpret statistics.

'I just had a poor series in '84 when the pressure was immense, but as a batsman you always try to separate the external pressures from the task in front of you, i.e., scoring runs. The irony is when you're losing games, the moment you walk out to bat as a captain you have the motivation and opportunity to do something about it. It just didn't happen for me that summer.'

Worse than Bodyline?

'When you bowl a bouncer at around 90 miles per hour, it doesn't come down with love. There is intent to make that batsman uncomfortable.' – Winston Davis

When Douglas Jardine led his England team, or Marylebone Cricket Club as it was then, on tour to Australia in 1932/33 he had devised a most ruthless plan with the intention of stopping Donald Bradman's prolific run-scoring and regaining the Ashes.

The story of how Jardine asked Harold Larwood and Bill Voce to bowl short-pitched deliveries aimed at the batsmen's bodies with fielders close in on the leg side has been well told. Jardine never liked the term Bodyline and always referred to it as 'leg theory'.

That he achieved his aim with a 4-1 series victory by defying the game's traditions around sportsmanship with a single-minded fearlessness rarely seen before or since was admirable in as much as he delighted a nation back home.

But in doing so he antagonised and upset another, for the Australian Cricket Board were so incensed by Jardine's tactics they threatened to boycott the 1934 tour of England if Jardine was still captain. Australian crowds had booed and barracked Jardine throughout the tour as their batsmen suffered multiple blows to the head and body.

Jardine, after taking the team to India the following year, eventually resigned and felt, understandably, like he had been hung out to dry by the English cricket authorities as they gradually railed against his tactics, despite their delight at the time of victory. The tour in 1934 went ahead without further political turmoil. Australia regained the Ashes 2-1.

So, what relevance does this background have to the 1984 summer? Well, quite simply, in the intervening years a subconscious acceptance of intimidatory fast-bowling tactics had been created and tolerated. Teams routinely selected fast bowlers to make life uncomfortable for their opponents.

Gone were the days of widespread condemnation and so we witnessed many episodes over the years of batsmen being hunted down by hostile fast bowling. As protective equipment became more sophisticated from the late 1970s and subsequently reduced batsmen's chances of serious injury, the practice of prolonged short-pitched deliveries became more common and less shocking, though it still disappointed the traditionalists.

Those pace bowlers would mostly hunt in pairs, occasionally as a trio. There was Dennis Lillee and Jeff Thomson; Fred Trueman and Brian Statham, who were joined by Frank 'Typhoon' Tyson in just the one Test match (that was lost in Adelaide); Neil Adcock and Peter Heine were enough of a handful as a pair; Keith Miller and Ray Lindwall were usually joined by Bill Johnston and later another left-armer, Alan Davidson; while Wes Hall and Charlie Griffith had enough firepower between them.

In more recent times, Wasim Akram and Waqar Younis supported an ageing Imran Khan, before firebrand Shoaib Akhtar supported an ageing Wasim Akram and Waqar Younis.

However, the four-pronged pace attack of the West Indies from the late seventies through to the early nineties was something else. Many observers would suggest the attack of Malcolm Marshall, Michael Holding, Joel Garner and Andy Roberts was the West Indies at their fearsome best. Before Marshall's emergence there was Colin Croft, the angriest of angry fast bowlers. After Roberts, in '84, there was the less rapid but no less accurate Eldine Baptiste, who played his part in the 5-0 trouncing of England.

Clive Lloyd is often credited, rightly, as the man who gave us the four-pronged pace attack. And who could blame him? He had seen his batsmen hammered by the pace of Lillee and Thomson in 1975/76 when they lost the series 5-1.

Then they were defeated in Trinidad in 1976 when India chased 406 to win against a West Indies team that included a trio of spin bowlers. Lloyd thought 'never again'. And he turned to pace. They didn't disappoint him.

This West Indies team had quality throughout the line-up with batsmen like Lloyd, Viv Richards and Gordon Greenidge. But many of their victories were based upon the fear factor created and sheer excellence of their pace bowlers as they went undefeated in Test series between 1980 and 1995.

As Jardine discovered, Lloyd and his team faced the inevitable backlash from those who felt the game of cricket was poorer for its use of four fast bowlers: some said this was boring for the sport as an entertainment; some said an over-indulgence on pace made over rates too slow; some said it created a graveyard for spin bowlers; some said the constant short-pitched tactics were overly intimidatory against batsmen and, subsequently, contravened the spirit of cricket.

'The man whose brainchild it was, Clive Lloyd, changed the shape and the flavour of West Indian cricket by his strategy of mass bombardment,' former *Wisden Almanack* editor David Frith wrote in *The Independent*. 'Winning was now everything.'

He added: 'The bursts of intimidation have been allowed by a succession of umpires who have steadfastly refrained from intervening. Their collective inaction has been explained away in a complexity of supposition: absence of either support or reassurance by the cricket authorities; or perhaps fear of physical reprisal by outraged fans ...'

Veteran English cricket writer John Woodcock wrote in *The Times*, having witnessed an especially and elongated sequence of hostile bowling from the West Indies on an uneven pitch at Sabina Park in 1986, when Richards had replaced Lloyd as captain. 'The longer the match went on, the less like a civilised game of cricket it became. Except on that evening of ill fame at Old Trafford in 1976, when (Brian) Close and John Edrich were subjected to such a disgraceful barrage by the West Indian fast bowlers, I think I have never felt it more likely that we should see someone killed.' It was 'cricket's equivalent to the Somme', he added.

Neutrals and certainly West Indians might wonder if these same writers were as incensed and outraged when Tyson was bouncing the Australians in 1954/55 or when Heine and Adcock were attacking the bodies of the New Zealanders in South Africa's ill-tempered series in 1961/62.

Or, more pertinently, when West Indian blood was spilled on Australian soil in 1975/76. Lloyd himself was hit on the jaw by Lillee in Perth and by Thomson in Sydney; Bernard Julien's thumb was broken; Kallicharran's nose was smashed by Lillee in Perth; most West Indian batsmen at some stage during the tour felt the pain of being hit by a cricket ball.

'That's the game,' Lloyd said during his reign as captain. 'It's tough. There's no rule about bowling fast. Batsmen must cope to survive. Short-pitched bowling is part of the quickie's equipment. He can't be too regulated, or he would lose the surprise element. The umpire can't tell a fast bowler that there should be only one short ball an over, because after that the surprise element is lost. Complaints come from batsmen ill-equipped to play the stuff. I am not sure that if every side had four fast bowlers of the quality we have, they wouldn't choose them or they'd leave them out because of what somebody says about over rates.

'If England, India or Australia had Marshall, Holding Garner and Baptiste, you think they'd decide to drop one or two of them? I don't believe they would. If they were dishing out the medicine I don't believe they would be talking about over rates. A lot of nonsense is talked about how fast bowling is killing cricket. How is it killing cricket?

'We have fast bowlers who get people out. That's what the game is all about and there's no reason why we should change because we keep beating teams.'

Lloyd's West Indies certainly bore the brunt of cricket's resentment towards aggressive bowling tactics purely because they employed them better than anyone, with greater results and were the best exponents. They were victims of their own success.

'Not many players took on the short ball then,' Lloyd added. 'We did, we didn't duck them. Clyde Walcott told me that Statham and Trueman bowled lots of short balls, but our guys used to hook. When I was captain our short ball tactics looked worse because not many people could play the hook shot very well and got into trouble.'

The likes of Frank Gilchrist, Patrick Patterson, Shoaib Akhtar, Shaun Tait – they all received extensive coverage, individually, for their frightening pace at times in their careers even if the quality of the overall package was not commensurate. But in 1984, and at other periods in this era, Lloyd's team had a world-class attack that gave no quarter in pace, accuracy or wicket-taking skill. They had all bases covered.

'Any team that had four fast bowlers of the quality they had would have been doing exactly the same,' said England opener Chris Broad.

Broad missed the first Test at Edgbaston in '84 and played in the remaining matches after replacing the injured Andy Lloyd. He therefore did not witness the most controversial episode of the series relating to West Indies' so-called intimidatory tactics.

Umpire Dickie Bird twice intervened to warn Marshall for overdoing his bouncers, at tailender Bob Willis and then Ian Botham, who was the best of friends with Viv Richards and friendly with Marshall, away from the heat of battle it must be said.

That friendship offset what might have become an ugly standoff as Botham advised Bird he didn't mind the tactics.

'Bird said something like "space the bouncers out",' Clive Lloyd recalled. 'I don't know what that means.'

He added: 'I could not agree with umpire Bird. Nor did he seem to be too clear about what he wanted us to do. Botham was at the wicket. He seemed quite prepared to take up the challenge, yet the umpire was warning us. I do not think at that point there was any question of us over-using the short-pitched delivery.'

Marshall was thankful for Botham's intervention as he felt it saved him from censure, had Bird deemed he was invoking laws around intimidation of the batsman.

'Ian Botham might well have saved me from disciplinary action and even, if it's not too far-fetched to suggest, being sent off in a Test match,' Marshall said in his autobiography *Marshall Arts*. 'I shall never know if that particular course of action was going through the mind of Dickie Bird as he issued me a warning for bowling too many bouncers at Edgbaston, but things were getting a bit bleak until the big man stepped in.

'Botham came in at number six and we all know how much he loves to hook and how he relishes the short ball. I stationed a man at long leg and the battle was on. He knew I was going to feed him a diet of short-pitched deliveries and I knew he would go for them. That was his style ... I must admit I felt bad about it but I was using every delivery available to me. While I concede it may have looked like I was trying to intimidate him with so many bouncers, it was a genuine tactic against a recognised batsman. I was pitching short to get him out, not to kill him.'

Marshall claimed he liked to get batsmen out 'fairly and squarely, not to maim or injure anyone', in the aftermath of Andy Lloyd's injury. 'I knew Lloyd's injury was not my fault and, to his credit, he acknowledged as much when I saw him later. All the West Indian players felt desperately sorry for the man, in his first big match.'

Jeffrey Dujon was obviously accustomed to taking the ball high above his head such was the regularity of the short ball, though he was also well known for taking some athletic, diving one-handed catches. Dujon may not have been an Alan Knott or an Ian Healy as far as technical keeping went, though he wasn't tested by the spinners as often, but to pace he was as good as any keeper there has ever been.

'People occasionally became a bit riled by our short balls, but that was normal,' Dujon commented. 'Yes, we bowled short quite often, especially when the conditions were amenable to it, but it was a tactic. We wanted to push them back so when we pitched the ball up they might have been a bit late or apprehensive about coming forward. I didn't think our bouncers or that tactic was excessive.'

Clive Lloyd's opposite number in '84, David Gower, was not offended by the West Indian tactics. He knew what to expect and probably wished, secretly, he had bowlers of the same menace to reciprocate the treatment. He detailed how it was not just the examination by pace that tested you as a batsman, but the skill level, too.

'With the abundance of fast bowling around in the Caribbean then, you seldom knew the challenge would be easy,' Gower said. 'Between them, the calypso spirit had been parked. Clive Lloyd had brought them all together, more than previous captains, while their Australian trainer Dennis Waite had made them fit. So, they had stamina, they had nous, good leadership and it all made for a brilliant team.

'When I look back on playing against all of them down the years, I would say Marshall was the best. Mikey (Holding) was express. Andy Roberts was very clever as well as being extremely quick at times. Andy, who they called 'The Professor', was the inventor of a lot of the tricks they used, such as cross-seam bouncers. There were different types of bouncers they bowled and that shows how they were thinking fast bowlers. Sometimes you saw a bouncer and thought, "Okay, I can hit that," and it went through before you saw it. Other times the bouncer skidded or was slower than you anticipated. That was good use of their skills.

'By '84, they had Eldine Baptiste, who was sharp, but just not as sharp as Holding, Marshall, Roberts, Garner, Croft and all. They also played the spinner that summer, of course.'

Paul Terry, who had his arm broken and effectively his Test career ended at Manchester by a Winston Davis bouncer, said it wasn't individual brilliance that made the West Indies pace attack so difficult but the relentlessness of the challenge.

'It was pretty awesome to go up against that bowling attack, in terms of understanding how tough it was,' Terry reflected. 'I certainly wouldn't say it was the most enjoyable experience of my life. Most of us would have had some success against one of their bowlers in county cricket but against all of them together was a very different proposition. The pressure was constant, constant, constant.'

Even Gordon Greenidge understood the challenge as he tested himself against his own bowlers in the nets. It is understandable to think the pacemen would 'go easy' on their own batsmen, but apparently not.

'Net practice was always a tense situation,' Greenidge said. 'Those guys gave no quarter whatsoever. You really had to be on your best behaviour during practice. The batters that liked to chatter and got under the skin of the fast bowlers seemed to bring another yard and a half out of them – so I kept quiet! But it was also a good situation because it primed you well for whatever you were going to receive out in the middle from the opposition.'

The challenge of facing the West Indies pace attack was hard enough for the best batsmen in world cricket, so consider then what the poor opposition tailender had to endure when going out to bat.

England's Richard Ellison faced them on his Test debut at The Oval and again in the return series in the Caribbean in 1986.

'It felt like an ordeal because it was relentless,' Ellison recalled with dread. 'Blinding pace from both ends! In county cricket you might survive Malcolm Marshall, but then from the other end it was light relief when Tim Tremlett, Cardigan Connor or Nigel Cowley came on. No disrespect to those guys but the West Indies fast bowlers were a different league.

'I faced Joel Garner at Folkestone playing for Somerset in one of my first Championship games (in 1981) and managed to score 61 not out. He was tough obviously, but it was much easier when you didn't have his mates coming at you from the other end like you did against the West Indies. There was no escape.'

Graeme Fowler said the gameplan was to play back most of the time as the majority of balls received were short, but he was equally conscious that the dangerous deliveries were the pitched-up ones. They were the ones that trapped the batsmen lbw, caught behind, bowled, whereas the short ones, he felt, were mainly just uncomfortable.

That was a clever tactic in itself as the bowlers were pushing the batsman back before the fuller delivery. And all this going on at around 90mph every ball. The concentration required was draining on batsmen. 'As I was walking off the field for the final time in the series,' recalled Fowler, 'an overwhelming feeling of relief came over me. I was in one piece. I hadn't been aware of this physical pressure until it was lifted.'

Although the West Indies did attract their share of negative media coverage and from the purist cricket supporter, unjustly or not, England all-rounder Derek Pringle believed they always played within the laws of the game and in the right spirit. They were just tough.

'They didn't overdo it unless they were on the defensive, in which case they probably did, but they were rarely on the defensive,' Pringle commented. 'You might get one pitched-up ball an over. Goochie used to say they bowl two half-volleys an hour so when they come you need to put them away, which is why he used a heavy bat to make sure he gave himself the best chance to do that.

'If you didn't exploit those rare loose balls, you were going to be limited to the odd single off the back foot. Fours were hard to come by unless you were a good hooker and, at that pace, the hook was always a dangerous shot.'

Dujon kept extensively to each of the main pace protagonists that preyed on batsmen in world cricket through the 1980s. Dujon, who never lost a series in the whole of his 81-Test career, detailed what made each of them unique.

Michael Holding: 'Mikey never really banged the ball into the pitch, he would just get the ball to kiss the surface and still come through at good pace though he wasn't as quick then in 1984 as he was before. He could get the ball to swing late and was always capable of giving the batsman a quick bouncer if he wanted to.'

Joel Garner: 'Later on in his career, we gave him the new ball and that seemed to re-energise him. He had been playing for Somerset so long that he knew what the conditions were like and he knew how to exploit them, especially with a new ball in his hand. He had a very good series in 1984.'

Malcolm Marshall: 'We had some very good assessors of batsmen and Malcolm was probably the best. He had great cricket-savvy, and we pooled all the information that we had and worked out a strategy. But there was always a Plan B.'

Winston Davis: 'He was deceptively quick. I played against him in the Caribbean and he was capable of bowling at two paces; he could surprise you with a very quick ball and I think that happened to Paul Terry. It got on to him quicker than he expected. He was wiry and didn't need a lot out of his run-up to bowl at good pace. Whereas someone like Malcolm needed that momentum so he preferred to sprint in. Winston had an uncomplicated action.'

Eldine Baptiste: 'Eldine did a wonderful job for us, keeping things tight with his discipline and he chipped in with some valuable wickets. I'm sure Eldine would have played a lot more if the depth of our pace bowling wasn't as strong as it was as Courtney Walsh was there too, before the likes of Patrick Patterson, Ian Bishop, Curtly Ambrose and Winston Benjamin came on the scene.

'At one point we could have fielded eight fast bowlers that would have made it into any team in the world. We had Wayne Daniel, Ezra Moseley, Sylvester Clarke, Tony Gray, and more.'

Patrick Patterson (who came on the scene from 1986): 'Patrick Patterson was the quickest I kept to. In '86 against England and a couple of times in Australia as well, he was like lightning. Malcolm was up in that bracket when he wanted to be. But keeping to Patto felt very different. When he got it right I have never seen a bowler swing a cricket ball at that pace. In Kingston against England, he bowled quickly and swung it and their batsmen just didn't have enough time to react to it.'

Here is another interesting account from a bowler who faced the West Indies attack in that series. Norman Cowans played in just the fourth Test at Old Trafford and would not generally bat higher than number nine for his county team Middlesex. But his recollection of facing Joel Garner, especially, in that match was fascinating for its detail as he summed up the challenge facing any batsman, no matter the number he came in.

'That match was the first time I had faced Garner and, although I was a tailender, I was amazed at Joel's bowling action,' Cowans said. 'He was bent at the waist in his run-up and by the time he came to his delivery stride it felt like this Big Bird was flying right over you. I had never faced anything like it, and I remember thinking, "How does any batsman face this bloke with any success?" And even if you cope against Joel, what about Marshall, Holding and Baptiste? It was relentless and you could never say you were *in* against them. You just hoped your openers could blunt them and take the shine off the ball but even with an old ball they found an extra yard (of pace) and were always *at* you.'

It feels right that one member of the pace attack of 1984, and that generation of West Indian pace in general, has the last word on this topic. Maybe he speaks for them all when detailing their challenge. They never once intended to hurt or injure any batsman, but if it happened it was part of the job and was never personal. Equally, if any batsman was naïve enough to rile the bowler, then he might expect to 'smell the leather'. One such example was Steve Waugh's confrontation with Curtly Ambrose in Trinidad in 1995, with his aggressive body language and verbals, which resulted in a vicious barrage of bouncers.

'There is a real possibility the batsman will get hit if he makes a bad decision and there have been times in my career that certain batsmen were antagonistic, and you would target him,' Winston Davis admitted. 'It was a way of getting even with them; they're trying to make you look small, after all.

'There are times with fast bowling when you are showing pure aggression towards the batsman. When you bowl a bouncer at around 90 miles per hour, it doesn't come down with love. There is intent to make that batsman uncomfortable.'

The Irony of Broad and Robinson

'Our England careers did kind of dovetail. It seemed to be him or me that got picked.' – Tim Robinson

'We did tend to replace each other in the team a lot rather than play together, which was unfortunate. Things worked out in strange ways a few times.' – Chris Broad

It's not often that someone would consider himself fortunate to have been overlooked for selection to the England Test team when his form merited selection. Yet Tim Robinson views his bad luck in 1984 as a lucky break, or a fortuitous signpost in time, and it's tough to question his rationale.

Instead, his Nottinghamshire opening partner Chris Broad was selected as a replacement for the injured Andy Lloyd in the Lord's Test and went on to have a solid but unspectacular series, which culminated in him being omitted for the winter tour to India, somewhat ruthlessly.

It was the start of a curious pattern that continued for the rest of the decade, whereby Broad and Robinson vied for a place against one another, as opposed to playing together. Robinson played 29 Tests between 1984 and 1989 and averaged 36.38. Broad featured in 25 Tests in the same period and averaged 39.54.

It could be argued they were England's best two openers in the 1980s, after Graham Gooch. Supporters of Geoffrey Boycott and Graeme Fowler may have a different view, but they were certainly ahead of many other openers who were tried out by England in the decade such as Bill Athey (averaged 22.97 in 23 Tests), Mark Benson (one Test in 1986), Wilf Slack (15.50 in three), Martyn Moxon (28.43 from ten), Kim Barnett (29.47 from four), Chris Smith (30.15 from eight), Tim Curtis (15.55 in five) and Chris Tavare (31.16 in his 18 Tests as an opener), among others. Andy Lloyd's Test career ended at Edgbaston in 1984 before it begun.

After the 1984 summer, Broad was replaced by Robinson, who went on to score 444 runs at an average of 63.42 in a triumphant five-match Test series in India that ensured his inclusion in the home Ashes of 1985. 'Robbo' extended that golden honeymoon period with a further 490 runs at 61.25, including 175 in the first Test at Headingley. Broad was treated harshly, no doubt, but it is interesting how selectorial decisions can make and break careers or just mould them differently to what the majority would expect to be right.

Nottinghamshire played Leicestershire at Grace Road in the match before Broad was called up, when England captain David Gower was playing for the Foxes. Robinson scored 171 in the first innings and 85 not out in the second. The bowling was not exactly weak with a recently retired Andy Roberts, along with England hopeful Jonathan Agnew and Test spinner Nick Cook in the Leicestershire attack.

It looked inevitable that Robinson would be the one to partner Fowler at the top of the England order, considering Lloyd's sickening injury sustained in the first Test. Robinson had also performed 12th man duties at Edgbaston so was clearly in the selectors' thoughts.

'When I look back there is no doubt that I was lucky *not* to get the call in '84,' Robinson said. 'You need a bit of luck or a break in professional sport and that may well have been mine. It allowed me to keep my powder dry and get selected for the India tour and then the Ashes in '85.'

Robinson's comment may sound like he lacked confidence in what he might have achieved. But most would see it as a realistic acceptance that going in to open against the West Indies in 1984 was more akin to attending your own funeral than an opportunity to build your international career.

In any case, Robinson's ambitions at that stage were all associated with winning trophies with his native county. Not playing for his country.

'I was a Notts lad, and I probably didn't have enough ambition then as my world was all about playing for Notts,' Robinson acknowledged. 'We had a successful side then with Ricey (Clive Rice), (Richard) Hadlee and the other boys so that felt enough for me. When I did finally get the call for the India tour, it felt like the cherry on the top.

'A few reporters mentioned that I had a good chance of playing in that West Indies series, but I didn't pay too much attention to it. Broady had a reputation as being very good against quick bowlers so, for the West Indies series, he was always going to be the one to get the nod.'

That Robinson followed his successful 1985 Ashes series with a tour to the West Indies enabled him to experience what he missed in '84 anyway. It wasn't something he would care to savour again. He scored 72 runs in four Tests at an average of 9. His struggles belatedly supported why the selectors opted for Broad in the first place at Lord's in '84.

'I was brought in as someone who could play fast bowling, yet I scored one fifty, while Allan Lamb got three hundreds,' Broad said. 'So, in the cold light of day as an opener I didn't do my job. Once you see the shine off the new ball you should go on and get a few more runs.

'But it was my first series, and I was inexperienced at that level. There were no coaches around and, if you were lucky, you might get some advice from a senior player. There wasn't any technical advice from anyone or analysts as you have now, so you were left to your own devices to work out a way to succeed against these guys.'

Broad initially adapted well to the challenge, as he soaked up 115 deliveries in two and a half hours at the crease for his 55, before he perished to a diving Jeff Dujon catch after nudging a quick Malcolm Marshall ball off his hip. He and Fowler combined in an opening partnership of 101.

A duck in the second innings was followed by more crease occupation in the third Test at Headingley where he again defied the fearsome pace attack for 117 balls in making a painstaking 32. He added 42 and 21 at Old Trafford and 39 in the second innings at The Oval. So, while there was just one half-century in his eight innings during the series, he demonstrated plenty of courage and a good technique to keep Marshall, Garner and co. at bay.

'Chris used to play Wayne Daniel very well when we played him in county cricket, and he always seemed to play quick bowling well generally, as he proved when he went to Australia in '86/87,' Mike Gatting said. 'He stood up to pace and bounce with great skill.'

The left-handed Broad followed on from his encouraging first series with an innings of 86 against Sri Lanka at Lord's at the end of the 1984 international summer. He faced 242 deliveries but if he thought he had sewn up his place for a winter tour to India, he had to think again.

A conversation with journalist Alan Lee in the sponsors' tent after the day's play caused him to wonder how certain his name was for the trip to the subcontinent. Lee suggested to Broad he had batted his way out of the squad. Whatever the reasons, Lee was right. When the tour squad was announced, Fowler and Robinson seemed to be the openers of choice with a third opener, Moxon, also named in the party.

'I was very angry, very upset,' Broad reflected. 'I didn't even get a phone call to tell me before the squad was announced. To find out on the radio that I wasn't going was very disappointing.'

Gower insists he wanted Broad in the party but was also desperate for the inclusion of Phil Edmonds, a left-arm spinner he rated highly, and Mike Gatting, a renowned quality player of spin bowling, so therefore felt he had already used up his bargaining chips when the squad was selected. Edmonds was not popular with the hierarchy, while Gatting had not made the most of many opportunities to that point, so it was difficult for a relatively new captain as Gower was to over-debate for his own choices.

'It was as simple as Tim was the better player of spin and Chris much the better player of pace bowling,' Gower explained. 'It was perceived that Chris would struggle against the spin and the tour party was chosen pretty much on that logic. Chris had every right to say, "I've been battling hard against the West Indies and deserve the chance to bat on flatter pitches against a very different bowling attack in the hope of getting some big scores."

'Where he was mighty unlucky was at the end of the season once we had made our selection, we had this three-day void before we announced the tour party. In that time Chris was impossible to reach and we didn't know where he had gone. I think he might have gone to Cornwall on holiday, but anyway he was out of range.

'Then on the day the squad was announced on the radio I had to play a benefit match and bumped into Chris where I had to uncomfortably say, "Sorry". That wasn't pleasant. You get used to dropping players if you are captain for any length of time, but you would normally explain to them why it's happened. Here, this wasn't the case.'

Broad found sympathy from some unlikely sources and, therefore, it was a huge compliment to his talent and steady progress that two of the best fast bowlers of all time should choose to sing his praises.

'The England selectors made a positive move by bringing in the Nottinghamshire left-hander Chris Broad for his solidity and courage, and he did well, persevered better than most,' Malcolm Marshall said. 'Quite why England banished him to the wilderness of county cricket (after the summer) I shall never know.

'The West Indian bowlers came to respect his single-minded determination and it will remain a mystery why, having done a competent and thorough job, he was dismissed as suddenly as he was selected. Someone in the England hierarchy obviously decided he wasn't good enough. After bowling at him in four Tests, I can only say I thought he deserved a better fate.'

New Zealand great Richard Hadlee, who obviously knew Broad well from their time together at Nottinghamshire, was equally bemused and disappointed for Broad that he missed the India tour.

'He did nothing wrong against the West Indies or Sri Lanka,' Hadlee commented. 'He and Fowler were thrown in at the deep end to open the innings and Chris went and scored a half-century on his debut. That takes some spirit. The pair never really failed all series, though they weren't a screaming success either. Nobody was. Having sweated it out against the most hostile attack in the world, Chris should have been rewarded with a place on the tour. He was shattered by the decision to leave him out and well he might be.'

Robinson, to use Hadlee's words, was a screaming success in India as he plundered 160 in only his second Test. With Gooch able to resume Test cricket after his South Africa tour ban the following summer, Robinson consolidated his position as Gooch's opening partner through to his horror series of the Caribbean in 1985/86.

Other openers were subsequently tried out in '86, but eventually the selectors returned to Broad for the Ashes tour in 1986/87, when he partnered Athey at the top of the order, not Robinson. Athey's contributions in that series were solid and helped to retain the Ashes urn, though his overall moderate record for England would suggest he was not in the same class as either of the Nottinghamshire openers.

The irony of how their Test careers were rarely concurrent for the most part is not lost on either of Robinson or Broad. They opened together in just three Tests and one of them, against Pakistan at Edgbaston in 1987, saw an opening partnership of 119.

'We did tend to replace each other in the team a lot rather than play together, which was unfortunate,' Broad acknowledged. 'Things worked out in strange ways a few times, like how I got picked for my debut just after Robbo scored a big hundred against Leicestershire.' Robinson added: 'Our England careers did kind of dovetail. It seemed to be him or me that got picked. I don't ever remember anyone speaking about the need for a left- and right-handed combination. They didn't seem to worry about that in those days.'

Gower reflected that having selected Robinson ahead of Broad for the 1984/85 India tour, it was hard on Broad that the selectors did not stand by the same theory when it came to choosing the tour squad to the Caribbean in 1985/86.

'With the comfort of hindsight, I do wonder why we didn't use the same logic that we used here and go back to Broady for the West Indies, knowing that Tim was likely to be susceptible (against the West Indies' quick bowling),' Gower conceded. 'I am kind of arguing against myself here because we kept Tim in the side for the Ashes in '85 after he did well in India, and he deserved to play.

'But maybe there was then a strong case to be as ruthless with Tim before the West Indies (in 1986) as we were with Chris before that India tour. I am speaking without knowing the evidence or Chris's numbers from the previous season in 1985 but selection is not always down to stats and sometimes it is just about having trust in a player to perform a certain role.'

Robinson, for his part, accepts the common thread that has existed for the last 40 years in that Broad was renowned to be a better player of pace and he more skilful against spin. But equally, he was quick to make the point that you don't play the amount of Test and first-class cricket as an opener that he did if you cannot handle pace and the bouncing ball. He feels this theory may have been skewed over the years, though he was happy to report that the rivalry for an England place between him and Broad was not as sour as was often made out.

'I could play, and I proved it against quicker bowlers like Imran Khan and the West Indies bowlers playing county cricket,' Robinson commented. 'I never thought I had a problem with pace. Yes, I struggled against the West Indies in '86 but they were a different kettle of fish.

'Ultimately, all this jostling for an England place didn't affect our relationship though lots got written about it. I had a lot more arguments with Derek Randall and Eddie Hemmings than I ever did with Chris Broad. My world was Nottinghamshire as opposed to the England setup. It wasn't anywhere near as bad a relationship as everyone thought.'

Bradman's Invincibles of 1948 v the West Indies of 1984 v Steve Waugh's Australians of 2001

Quite simply, there is no right or wrong answer about the best cricket team of all time because these teams have never or will never play each other. Opinions are just that – opinions, they are not right answers; times change so much and that makes it difficult to compare eras, and such exercises are ultimately meaningless.

However, it is still fun and fascinating to indulge in some educated debate about which team would rule the world if they were around at the same time. The above three teams do seem to be the most likely and fitting of all Test teams to belong to such debate. There will always be someone who considers another team from another era worthy, but these three would generally meet the consensus.

The West Indies won a then-record 11 Tests in a row between March and November 1984. They smashed all-comers. This was possibly the greatest period of the greatest team.

The bigger picture was that between 1980 and 1995, the West Indies went a record 29 successive series without defeat (the next longest sequence is 16 series by the Australian team of 2001 to 2005); a record 27 Test matches without defeat between January 1982 and December 1984, and eventually beat all the usual opponents home and away.

The 1948 Australians, unbeaten in 25 Tests between the first post-war Test in 1946 to February 1951, almost achieved a whitewash of England that summer. The teams drew in Manchester as the fourth day washout meant neither team could force a result, after Denis Compton's brilliant 145 not out and Alec Bedser's four wickets gave England a first-innings lead of 142.

Australia, 1948: This team was dominated by the runs of their captain and talisman Donald Bradman, while there was the middle-order general Lindsay Hassett and the great left-hander Neil Harvey was emerging. Openers Arthur Morris and Sydney Barnes were both greats of their day and finished their Test careers with mighty impressive averages (Morris 46 and Barnes 63 from his brief 13-match career). The wicketkeeper Don Tallon was highly rated by many of that era. The seamers Ray Lindwall, Keith Miller and Bill Johnston gave them a cutting edge, but their lack of a great spin bowler of the ilk of Bill O'Reilly or Clarrie Grimmett who went before, or Shane Warne who came many years after, slightly diminishes their legacy.

West Indies, 1984: Eight of the players from the nucleus of this team would generally be regarded as all-time greats: cavalier opening batsmen Gordon Greenidge and Desmond

Haynes, middle-order powerhouses Viv Richards and Clive Lloyd, wicketkeeper Jeffrey Dujon and fast bowlers Malcolm Marshall, Joel Garner and Michael Holding. Three of the others from '84 still played key roles in the 5-0 demolition of England, as number three batsman Larry Gomes was a candidate to be player of the series.

Australia, 2001: Although they lost 2-1 in India in 2001 after taking the lead, they had already made a serious mark on the world by then. That opening win in Mumbai in February 2001 was their 16th consecutive Test victory dating back to October 1999. The bowling attack was dominated by leg-spinner Shane Warne and seamer Glenn McGrath, and well supported by Jason Gillespie and Brett Lee. Openers Matthew Hayden and Michael Slater (soon to be replaced by Justin Langer) gave their innings early impetus, while the middle order was stuffed with reliable run-scorers like Mark Waugh, Ricky Ponting, Steve Waugh, Damien Martyn and wicketkeeper-batsman Adam Gilchrist. Only a generous declaration by stand-in captain Gilchrist allowed England to reach the unlikely but not impossible target of 315 at Headingley in 2001 to avoid a whitewash, yet they still went down 4-1 to Australia in the Ashes.

When author Roland Perry released a book titled *Bradman's Best*, in which 'The Don' selected his greatest XI of all time and explained his choices, he included himself and three other team-mates from his 1948 Ashes side, Arthur Morris, Ray Lindwall and Don Tallon.

Here are the thoughts and opinions from a collection of players from the 1984 series, and a few others, on the whole debate of 'Who's the greatest'.

Allan Border (talking about the West Indies, in that mid-1980s period): 'In my humble opinion, they're the best side ever assembled. Any side with Bradman in it has to be considered one of the best ever, but they had a relentless pace barrage over a 15-year period, plus a pretty awesome batting line-up and fielding side. If you put the whole lot together, it's a pretty compelling argument (that they're the best ever).'

Garfield Sobers (interviewed in 2000): 'I didn't see Bradman, and I came into Test cricket towards the end of Keith Miller's and Ray Lindwall's careers. They were still pretty good bowlers, but it is hard for me to make any great comment on them because they were on their way out. However, I still feel privileged to have played against them. I was more of a bowler in those days so batted down the order, but I did open the innings in one Test match in that 1954/55 series and I can tell you that it was a lot different facing Keith and Ray at the top of the order than lower down. I can only echo the words of many others that Keith Miller was a great all-rounder, if not the greatest.

'Neil Harvey, Arthur Morris and Bill Johnston were other greats from that Australian team. I always liked to watch Arthur bat; I thought that if I had to model myself on any batsman, I would like it to be Arthur, because of his movements and the way he got behind the ball. Neil was a brilliant player too, very exciting and could be a destroyer in the middle order. I was lucky to see those players.

'Not long after I retired (in 1974), the West Indies discovered a battery of great pace bowlers. People like Michael Holding, Andy Roberts, Colin Croft, Joel Garner, Malcolm Marshall and later on Courtney Walsh and Curtly Ambrose. They made a very big impact because there had never been anything like it. They certainly shocked the world, and it took the world years to recover.

'We had about seven (fast bowling) greats from which you could pick four or five that would beat the world. It was very unfortunate for some that they all came along together because the likes of Wayne Daniel, Franklyn Stephenson and Sylvester Clarke – who were all quick and very good – didn't get much of a chance.

'(As regards Australia 2001), someone who is called great from today's game is Shane Warne, but I have got my reservations about Shane. I think he is a great bowler, but I'm not sure how well he compares with spinners overall. I think people get carried away with this man's ability as he hardly ever bowled a good googly. To me, Shane is a great turner of the ball, and I like his aggressive attitude, I love the way he attacks batsmen and I give him 100 per cent for that as not enough spinners bowl with that approach, but in my estimation Subhash Gupte (of India) was a far better spinner ... I accept Shane Warne is a great of his era but I'm not sure about overall.'

Frank Keating (journalist who saw Bradman's Invincibles): 'They were great in 1948, but the greatest of all sides? Well, where's the spinner? Johnson (seven Test wickets with off-breaks, at a whacking 61 average) and the leggie Ring (one Test, 1-44) were no shakes at all. Can you be a truly great side, in a cricketing sense, without a half-decent spinner?

'To be sure, Clive Lloyd's irrepressible 1984 "blackwash" side had off-spinner (and ace fieldsman) Roger Harper slipping in with 13 wickets, a potent bonus to add to 29 from Garner, 24 by the slippery whippet Marshall and 15 by the classicist Holding. Useful, after a resplendent batting order: Greenidge, Haynes, Richards, Lloyd, Gomes, Dujon. Yep, the 1948 Australians could well have been Big Brothered had they played in 1984.'

Ian Botham: 'That West Indies team in '84 is the best side I ever played against, and I feel the West Indies of the mid-1980s in general was the best team that has ever played Test cricket. People say they didn't have a (world-class) spinner, but they didn't need one with those four guys. They were a magnificent team. It was a privilege to play against them.'

Michael Holding: 'I couldn't say if the '84 team itself was the best ever, but I know for about four or five years around that period we were almost untouchable.'

Allan Lamb: 'That West Indies team in '84 was by far the best team I have seen. The Aussie attack I faced in my first series in 1982/83 was good but less potent than what the West Indies had in 1984 purely because they never had four fast guys coming at you all the time. It would have been like England having four Mark Woods in the 2023 Ashes series. If they had four Woods they would have blown Australia away, just like West Indies blew us and Australia away back in our day, too. Even when Australia had the best team around with McGrath and Warne, that 1984 West Indies team would have blown them away, too.

When you have four or five quick bowlers like they had, there's no hiding place for opposition batsmen. It's as difficult as can be. Out of all my Tests against the West Indies, we only won one game, in Jamaica. That was it. They were awesome, just brilliant.'

Derek Pringle: 'I think the Aussies in 2001 might have had a better bowling attack than this '84 team. I think the West Indies had an even better bowling attack in '88 with the introduction of (Curtly) Ambrose, (Courtney) Walsh and (Patrick) Patterson along with Malcolm Marshall. In '84, Joel was probably just over his peak at that stage, Michael Holding certainly was and Malcolm was on the way up. I'm not sure the two all-rounders (Harper and Baptiste) would have got in the team in '88. But when you look at the batting, Gordon Greenidge, Desmond Haynes and Viv were probably in their pomp then. All things considered that '84 side was a daunting team and it's hard to say any other side would have been better.'

Chris Broad: 'I obviously didn't see Bradman's team, while I played against the 1984 West Indies and saw a great deal of Steve Waugh's Australia side.

'A lot rested on the shoulders of McGrath and Warne in the Steve Waugh team. I don't see there's much difference in the batting. Hayden, Langer, Ponting and the Waugh brothers were a quality batting line-up, and stacks up to Greenidge, Haynes, Richards, Gomes and Lloyd. If Australia hadn't had Warne and McGrath, results would have been very different. But with that West Indies team they seemed to have reserves of fast bowlers who could come in and take wickets. Therefore, I would put the West Indies team down as a stronger all-round side.

'I faced the West Indies in '88 when they were still mighty strong, but the '84 attack was better because they had more experience. Curtly Ambrose and Joel Garner were quite similar given the heights they bowled from, Courtney Walsh was around in '84 but never played, Patrick Patterson was genuinely fast in '88 but raw. They were undoubtedly a good team in '88 but I'd say the '84 team was better because of that superior bowling attack.'

David Gower: 'The press conferences were quite tough throughout the '84 series, but at the end of Old Trafford, glimpses of humanity started to break through from the press. For half an hour, after I had basically said, "Well, what more can we do against this great team?" our assembled press pack were quite sympathetic. Their tone became more like, "How are you finding it? We do sympathise. They're very good, aren't they?" When you are 4-0 down with a match to go, as captain you're up against it, so their understanding and pretty much saying they were not going to crucify me, that was very good news and was helpful.

'I had the misfortune to captain England to two 5-0 series defeats to the West Indies and I still say '84 was the toughest series I ever played because it was like being hit by a steam train. In '86, after winning the Ashes the year before, I didn't necessarily have hopes of beating the West Indies in the Caribbean, but I did at least hope we would compete more than in '84. The biggest disappointment about '86 was that even though we ended up in the same place, with that stark scoreline of 5-0, we should have been a better team and should have made that series score better than it ended up. In '84, the gulf between the teams was just too great. For that whole decade, the West Indies were almost unbeatable.'

Mike Gatting: 'They were definitely at their strongest in '84 purely for the all-round quality of their players from one to 11. That bowling attack never seemed to have a weakness. You had to be at your best every day against that West Indies team and, unfortunately, I wasn't at my best once.'

Richard Ellison: 'The West Indies then were almost unbeatable. I didn't play many Tests against the West Indies but facing them was still the toughest challenge of my whole career, with bat and ball. I think they belong to the same league as Bradman's Invincibles and Steve Waugh's team in later years. It was relentless as a batsman against them, and as a bowler there was no hiding place either with all those world-class batsmen they had in their ranks.'

Paul Terry: 'The West Indies were the greatest cricketers going around in '84 and I still don't think we have seen anything like it since. There have been teams with bowlers like Wasim and Waqar, Warne and McGrath, Curtly and Courtney, but these guys were formidable throughout the line-up. They were a fearsome, tough bunch as a team and didn't say much out there on the field, but once you met them away from the action you saw what good guys they were.'

Neil Foster: 'The West Indies were the best team I ever saw or played against, without a doubt. There was no weakness. All their fast bowlers were fast and offered different things and weren't just quick but were high quality bowlers who just kept coming at you. They batted aggressively and with depth. If they started well they could take games away from you very quickly. It felt like self-preservation most of the time, whether you were protecting your bowling figures when you bowled or your safety when you batted.'

Roger Harper: 'The 1984 team was the best that I was ever involved with. Without a doubt. That team which beat India from such a difficult situation in '83 then went on to show it wasn't a fluke by doing it again at Lord's in '84. That just says it all. The team had all-round strength in depth, in bowling, batting but especially in the fielding department. The standard of catches that were routinely taken was outstanding. The credit for that must go to the captain who really drove us in practice to those high standards. He told us over and again that we won't be able to beat teams if we don't take our catches. We also went to the subcontinent, especially India and Pakistan, and won when other teams struggled to do that.'

Jeff Dujon: 'The 1984 side is the best team I ever played in – no question about it. I'm the only one who has never lost a Test series having played 81 Tests, so I must have played in a very good team! In '84 we had every base covered and won the series in all departments, hands down. We had some great series in Australia as well but that England series in '84 was almost certainly the most dominant that we were at any point in that era.'

Courtney Walsh: 'We were coming into our best form in '84 having already beaten Australia at home that year and after losing the World Cup the year before. After the World Cup the guys were closer as team-mates, were hungrier for success and probably wanted to prove to the world that the World Cup loss wasn't the start of something bad but the opposite, as they were more ambitious than ever.'

Gordon Greenidge: 'We were strong in '84 but we were at other times also. It might not have been 5-0 in 1976 but you have got to look at the whole package of the tour. We played excellent cricket in that beautiful, hot summer as well. The manner of how we played our cricket was exciting and very polished and courageous. We played the way we wanted to play and were attacking right the way through.'

Andy Lloyd: 'You must appreciate just how good this West Indies team was. Pitch conditions always make a huge difference to any cricket match. If you are in Sydney and you are playing Australia with Shane Warne in their team, as opposed to Roger Harper for the West Indies side, then Shane Warne will win that match for his team invariably. But if you play pretty much anywhere else – whether it's Melbourne, Perth, Edgbaston, Jamaica – the fast bowlers win you the game quicker than the spin bowler(s). And they had the best fast-bowling attack in the world for a long time.'

Paul Downton: 'In '81 the West Indies had Roberts, Holding, Garner, Croft, and Marshall also played the last Test, so I would say that bowling attack was at least as strong as what they had in 1984 if not stronger. That was a challenging proposition in their own conditions, though we played on some decent batting wickets and some of our guys scored centuries. We lost two and drew two, we weren't blown out of the water like we were in '84, when the pitches were slower, lower, and therefore harder to bat on. We were a more experienced batting side in '81 with Gooch and Boycott opening and with the likes of Willey and Gower in the middle order.

'Ultimately at that time we weren't good enough, but the West Indies were an exceptional side. Most of their players felt like it was a home series because of all the county cricket they played between them. The support they had around the grounds was huge, especially at The Oval. So, these were some of the best players in the world playing in conditions that were very familiar to them. County cricket was a finishing school for them. Their inner belief and confidence was second to none and even when they were in a spot of bother, they found a way to succeed. Psychologically they had a real hold on us.'

A Statement Extending
Beyond Cricket

'Cricket was common ground and helped break down
barriers and showed why sport is such a great thing in
bringing people together, when society can be divisive in
so many ways.' – Norman Cowans

England fast bowler Norman Cowans was an integral member of the great Middlesex team of the 1980s and played in the fourth Test of the 1984 series against the West Indies, and 19 Tests in total. He was born in Enfield, Jamaica and emigrated to England when aged 11.

His mother had shifted to England when he was still a baby and he was raised by his grandfather and great aunt, until his mother later sent for him. Young Norman therefore moved to Harrow in 1972 with his strong Jamaican accent and had to adjust to a radically different culture.

Given this background, Cowans understood better than most what impact the West Indies cricket team had on the Afro-Caribbean population in the United Kingdom. The social and cultural effect of Clive Lloyd's successful team was ultimately significant. Two World Cup wins in 1975 and 1979 and global domination in Test cricket that culminated with the 5-0 series win in 1984, often referred to as a 'blackwash', did wonders for morale among West Indian expatriates in the UK, as Cowans explained.

'Given the way that West Indians were treated when they came to England, they didn't have anything to lift them from the depression and gloom of their situation,' Cowans said. 'It was supposed to be a shift to a better and more prosperous life, but there was no respect for them, and they were treated inhumanely a lot of the time with no adequate housing or employment available to many of them, most of whom were well-educated people.

'There was nothing positive about the way they were portrayed in the media or on the television. They were treated badly in the streets, they were basically not welcomed as they thought they would be.

'So, when the West Indies came over to tour England in the sixties, seventies and especially the eighties, the West Indian people living there looked at them like they were representing them as a people. West Indies' visits lifted their spirits and seemed to give them more respect on the street and a better profile and identity than before. Cricket gave West Indians something to shout about and brought them together with their English friends over a drink in the pub.

'Cricket was common ground and helped break down barriers and showed why sport is such a great thing in bringing people together, when society can be divisive in so many ways. I saw it myself when I played club cricket, with English, West Indians, Indians and Pakistanis all playing together through sport and you can't appreciate just how magnificent that was at the time for people who had very little else to celebrate in their lives.

'We started to see people like Trevor McDonald, who was from Trinidad and a cricket lover, working on the TV. In so many ways West Indian people suddenly started to feel integrated and a part of British society through cricket, when they once did not and had felt ostracised and unwelcome. Cricket, and particularly the West Indies team's exploits, was a great instrument in bridging so many gaps.'

In terms of that cultural celebration or self-congratulation amongst West Indians in England, it was much needed after the social problems emanating from West Indian communities that had broken out, such as the Brixton and Handsworth riots of 1981, which resurfaced in the future. Nobody ever suggested cricket provided a fix for these deep-rooted issues, but it certainly helped bring smiles when there had been snarls. The so-called 'blackwash' achievement provided West Indians, whether first or second generation, with a confidence and self-respect that might not always have existed. Cricket was a great leveller as English people, and even other nationalities globally, looked at the West Indies team as great ambassadors for the way they went about the sport, and they enjoyed and appreciated how they had taken the game to new heights.

'I would obviously like to have played more in that series than one match, but that wasn't just because it was the West Indies. I always wanted to play against the best and West Indies were the best then,' added Cowans.

The impact of the 1984 series on the public was huge, in a summer when the England national football team had not managed to qualify for the European Championship so focus was on cricket more than it might otherwise have been.

England wicketkeeper Paul Downton played in all five Test matches and he felt that the passionate support for the West Indies from British West Indians in and around the grounds was a huge motivation for their team to perform well.

'This West Indies team really felt like they were representing their people in England and that gave them an added hard-nosed edge to their play,' Downton commented. 'They were all good blokes individually but as a team they had a very hard edge to them and it seemed like they were more motivated to beat England, especially in England, than they would have been against any other side.'

Former England batsman Denis Compton was in awe of the level that the West Indies were playing at and wrote in his national newspaper column: 'What a battering for our cricketers. I cannot remember ever seeing an England side so utterly humiliated, as the West Indians took our bowlers by the scruff of the neck. The irritating thing was that at times they seemed to be toying with us.'

The effect of results on the people in England and even back home in the Caribbean was not lost on their captain Clive Lloyd: 'The pattern of my captaincy of the West Indies team was to a great extent dictated by the fact that the game is so terribly important for us in the Caribbean. It is much more than a game. It carries with it all sorts of aspirations and hopes of West Indian people. The key to the West Indies captaincy is realising all that.'

Through the Looking Glass

*'Clive was more man to man when talking to people
and had a different, calmer personality. Viv was quite
demonstrative when pointing out what he wanted from
the guys. They were two different types of personality,
but I don't think it changed the dynamic on the field.'* –
Jeffrey Dujon

In 1984, it would have been almost incomprehensible to
think that West Indian dominance in world cricket would
end in just over a decade. More shocking would have been
the thought that the West Indies would not even be one
of the powerhouses of the Test arena a further decade on.
But happen it did.

So many players have spoken in detail over subsequent
years that it was the negligence of the West Indies Cricket
Board (as it was known then) for not reinvesting the fees it
earned from touring the world into grass roots, academies
and infrastructure across the Caribbean to ensure the
ongoing development of quality cricketers.

Others simply believe these things go in cycles and
no one country has a divine right to always be on top of
the world and dominating. In fairness, the complicated
political aspect of West Indies cricket is one that no

other cricket board has to deal with whereby different governments across the region all have a stake in West Indies cricket. Therefore, it can be challenging for major investment decisions to be made.

The relatively sudden fall from grace has been painful, though the signs were becoming evident. England, as an example of their progress, lost another series 5-0 to the West Indies in 1986, then 4-0 in 1988. But it was 2-1 in the Caribbean in 1990, 2-2 in 1991 in England, 3-1 in 1994, 2-2 in 1995 and 3-1 in 1998 until England finally started to win series consistently from 2000, when they won 3-1, followed by a 3-0 triumph in the West Indies and then 4-0 in England in 2004 and 3-0 in 2007.

The tables had well and truly turned. In fact, South Africa beat the West Indies 5-0 in their five-match series in 1998/99, even with several West Indian legends among their ranks such as Courtney Walsh, Curtly Ambrose, Brian Lara, Shivnarine Chanderpaul and Carl Hooper – here was yet more evidence that the overall effectiveness of 'team' is always more important than the calibre of individuals. The same scoreline occurred once more two years later in Australia.

The England and Wales Cricket Board implemented an overseas academy programme to better prepare burgeoning talent and began a central contracts system from 2000 to ensure more control of the schedules of their best players. Results seemingly reflected the added investment and they regained the Ashes five years later.

Apart from the odd flicker of positivity, West Indies have remained in the doldrums of Test cricket since they lost their unofficial world champion crown to Australia in 1995.

They have won Twenty20 World Cups in 2012 and 2016 and the 50-over Champions Trophy in 2004, as the shorter formats have appeared to better suit the talent they have had in recent years such as Dwayne Bravo, Chris Gayle, Kieron Pollard and Sunil Narine.

But the return to prolonged glory in Test cricket currently appears to be a long way off.

The new Cricket West Indies board has a difficult task to insist their best players are always available for international cricket against the crowded backdrop of global franchise tournaments that can make overnight millionaires of their players.

The balancing act of temporarily releasing players from board contracts for franchise cricket across the world is challenging as in an ideal world they would prefer more control over their own cricketers to stay fit, fresh, and available to play always for the West Indies. Yet that attitude almost seems naïve nowadays.

It is maybe the modern-day version of how West Indies' best cricketers took off for Australia in the late 1970s to play in Kerry Packer's revolutionary and lucrative World Series Cricket. The major difference is that Packer cricket was short-lived, and the legends soon returned to play for the West Indies after two seasons in Australia. The current issue appears to be here to stay and is likely to get worse before it improves.

Gordon Greenidge, one of the stars of the 1984 summer and indeed a true batting great in historic terms, is not overly shocked that the West Indies' demise has been lengthy.

'I am surprised in one sense and not in another,' he said, reflecting on West Indies' progress over the last two decades. 'The mentality of the players has changed and is still changing. The behaviour of the administrators changed – not all for the better; a combination of both needs to improve. Players now are dictating the way things should be, but I don't see players making any major difference towards the success of the team. Yet they argue about non-cricket things (inferring they are more interested in money matters than cricket matters). Players are still dedicated but more towards the one-day games than Test match cricket. I am not blaming them, just stating a fact. If people can go out there and get paid more for less work they will do it.'

The only player on the 1984 tour whose career lasted long enough to witness the modern-day version of the West Indies team was Courtney Walsh. The Jamaican fast bowler never played a Test in '84 but learned a lot from the legends he shared a dressing room with. He later combined in what became one of the most famous new-ball partnerships with Curtly Ambrose. Walsh retired in 2001 when it was clear that his beloved West Indies was nowhere near the fierce unit it had been when he came into the squad in the mid-eighties.

'It's hard to compare different teams because things are so different,' Walsh said, 'but on a general point it was clear that for the youngsters on that 2000 tour of England, and then when we went to Australia, that there were not the same number of mentors around to help them like I had around me in 1984.

'I did as much as I could to pass on to youngsters the lessons that I had learned, especially to the younger fast bowlers who came into the team. But passing on advice and guidance is one thing, then it is up to that young cricketer to use that advice and implement it or adapt it to their own game as best they can.'

If the long-term future for the West Indies from 1984 was a bleak one, at least the short-term future was much brighter. They lost only five Test matches over the next five years.

First, in 1984/85, Clive Lloyd led his champions into one final Test series against Australia before he handed over the reins to Viv Richards. Like on the England tour, they took an unassailable 3-0 lead to complete yet another series victory before a draw and their first Test defeat in three years. In 1984/85, they were spun out by leg-spinner Bob 'Dutchie' Holland, who took ten wickets in the match.

'We were gutted when we lost that fifth Test to Australia in Sydney,' Walsh added. 'Everyone wanted to do well for themselves and the West Indies obviously, but we also wanted to do well for Clive because of what he had done for West Indies cricket and for the way he had been a father figure to so many of us.'

Jeffrey Dujon soon detected, once the squad returned to the Caribbean for a home series with New Zealand, that the dynamic felt a little different without Lloyd in charge and with the more animated, outwardly passionate Richards leading the side.

'In the dressing room there was a difference as there were a few personality clashes that became noticeable, just because there was a different leadership style,' Dujon revealed. 'But on the field, it was a different matter, it was business as usual.

'Clive was more man to man when talking to people and had a different, calmer personality. Viv was quite demonstrative when pointing out what he wanted from the guys. They were two different types of personality, but I don't think it changed the dynamic on the field.'

One victim from the 1984 English summer was Eldine Baptiste. He didn't play in Australia or again actually until his farewell Test in 1990. He retired with ten Tests to his name and ten victories.

'Lloydy spoke to me when we went to Australia and said if the wickets have pace and bounce, he would play the extra fast bowler (Courtney Walsh) but if they were flat then I would play,' Baptiste revealed. 'I accepted it then as what was best for the team was okay by me. But I didn't realise I wouldn't play another Test for so long. It puzzled me. I got into the best team in the world by bowling the best batsmen out in our regional cricket. But it never helped me.'

Quite simply the arrival of yet more pace-bowling talent off the seemingly never-ending assembly line did for Baptiste. As well as Walsh and Davis, Patrick Patterson soon emerged, before the likes of Tony Gray, Winston Benjamin, Ian Bishop and Ambrose.

By early 1986, England had survived a run-frenzied draw with Sri Lanka at Lord's in '84, won a series in

India with a new-look team on the winter tour, and then regained the Ashes in 1985 by a scoreline of 3-1, after Graham Gooch and John Emburey had returned from their bans. Gower joked dryly on the balcony at The Oval during a television interview with Peter West that, 'I am sure the West Indies are quaking in their boots,' several months out from their tour to the Caribbean. It was a tongue-in-cheek throwaway line and was in no way on the same level as Tony Greig's 'I want to make them grovel' comment in 1976, but it still was a one-liner that the media were able to feed to the West Indians and perhaps created added motivation if they ever needed it. History tells us the series ended 5-0, again. The West Indies were largely the same as in '84 though Patterson had come in for Baptiste and Richie Richardson for Lloyd, while Walsh, Roger Harper and Carlisle Best played bit-part roles.

England were beaten by ten wickets in just three days in the first Test at Sabina Park, dismissed for 159 and 152 on what was a lightning-fast glass-like pitch that behaved inconsistently. Of course, England's bowlers were generally slower and therefore the same hazards were not a problem for the West Indies batters.

'The wickets were lethal,' Allan Lamb recalled. 'The Sabina Park wicket was the quickest I ever played on, and it had a ridge. It was tough. There was no hangover from '84, everybody wanted to score runs and take wickets, but the plan for the whole Test match wasn't there.

'There was stuff going on in the background, which never helped. We weren't allowed to train at the grounds, we could only play there. So practising was a nightmare. And we had the guys back from the rebel tour, Gooch, Emburey, Willey et cetera, so there was a lot of chanting from the locals. They'd shout, "Go back to South Africa" and all that. And the West Indies, I think, got a bit more motivated by those guys being out there.'

The emergence of the 24-year-old Jamaican Patterson created quite a stir as his pace was of a level most had not encountered previously. He had played for Lancashire in 1984 and 1985 though the consensus among the England players was that he was not bowling 95 miles per hour in the shires.

'Bloody hell he was quick,' Richard Ellison recalled, 'but at times he didn't know where the ball was going. It was just pure speed. He was quick, quick, quick.'

'Patterson's 7-24 against Guyana in the Shell Shield early in 1986 put him on Viv Richards' radar and when he had Richards caught when playing for Leeward Islands he was in. Jamaican wicketkeeper Dujon regards Patterson as the quickest he ever kept to.

It was a series that never worked out as England had hoped. Gooch, Emburey and Willey were back and Gower had his preferred spin attack of Emburey and Middlesex team-mate Phil Edmonds. And the young Glamorgan pace bowler Greg Thomas was supposedly going to fight fire with fire. There was more optimism than in 1984 but it was the same old story.

'I struggled terribly against the West Indies in '86 but they were on another level,' opening batsman Tim Robinson admitted. 'There was just no respite. When Viv had enough of Marshall and Garner, it was Patterson and Holding – Courtney Walsh couldn't get in the side.

'But I just feel fortunate to have played against that team because they have got to be one of the best Test sides ever. They were formidable. After we won in India and then beat Australia, that series was supposed to be a showdown between the best two sides in the world, but it wasn't a great showdown!'

Acknowledgements

Thank you to all those people who generously offered their time to be interviewed. They include Eldine Baptiste, Chris Broad, Norman Cowans, Winston Davis, Paul Downton, Jeffrey Dujon, Richard Ellison, Neil Foster, Mike Gatting, David Gower, Gordon Greenidge, Roger Harper, Michael Holding, Allan Lamb, Andy Lloyd, Clive Lloyd, Vic Marks, Geoff Miller, Pat Pocock, Derek Pringle, Tim Robinson, Paul Terry, Don Topley, Courtney Walsh and Julian Wyatt. And to Lord Ian Botham for the foreword.

Bibliography

Birmingham Central Library newspaper archive and research facilities.

Fowler, G., *Absolutely Foxed* (Simon & Schuster, 2016)

Garner, J., *Big Bird Flying High* (Arthur Baker, 1988)

Hadlee, R.J., *At The Double: The Story of Cricket's Pacemaker* (Stanley Paul, 1985)

The Independent, David Frith quotes on the West Indies' pace-bowling tactics

Keating, F., Quote on 1948 Australia v 1984 West Indies (*Wisden Cricket Monthly*, 1998)

Lloyd, C.H., *The Authorised Biography* (Granada Publishing, 1985)

Marshall, M.D., *Marshall Arts* (Queen Anne Press, 1987)

Sydenham, R.N., Interview with Gordon Greenidge in *Back Spin* magazine

Sydenham, R.N., Garry Sobers interview in *In A League of Their Own* (DB Publishing, 2009)

Wisden Almanacks 1984, 1985

Other source material

CODE Sports, Allan Border quote
CricketArchive.com for general statistics and research
ESPN Cricinfo for general statistics and research
The Times, John Woodcock quotes on the West Indies
    pace-bowling tactics